the series on school reform

Patricia A. Wasley
Bank Street College of Education

Ann Lieberman
NCREST

Joseph P. McDonald
New York University

SERIES EDITORS

This series also incorporates earlier titles in the Professional Development and Practice Series

Charter Schools: Another Flawed Educational Reform?

Seymour B. Sarason

TEACHERS
COLLEGE
PRESS

Teachers College, Columbia University
New York and London

For Julie, Paul, and Nathaniel
Who successfully created a new setting

Published by Teachers College Press, 1234 Amsterdam Avenue, New York, NY 10027

Library of Congress Cataloging-in-Publication Data

Sarason, Seymour Bernard, 1919–
    Charter schools : another flawed educational reform? / Seymour B.
Sarason.
        p.   cm. — (The series on school reform)
    Includes bibliographical references.
    ISBN 0-8077-3785-2 (cloth : alk. paper). — ISBN 0-8077-3784-4
(paper : alk. paper)
    1. Charter schools—United States.   2. Education and state—United
States.   3. Educational change—United States.   I. Title.
II. Series
    LB2806.36.S27   1998
    371.01—dc21   98-11732

ISBN 0-8077-3784-4 (paper)
ISBN 0-8077-3785-2 (cloth)

Printed on acid-free paper

Manufactured in the United States of America

05 04 03 02 01 00 99 98   8 7 6 5 4 3 2 1

Contents

Preface

Charter schools are the most radical educational reform effort in the post World War II era in that states encourage and permit these schools to be created exempt from burdensome, stifling, innovation-killing features of the culture of existing systems. One does not ordinarily associate "radical" with state and federal initiatives in the educational arena, but the fact is that the charter school movement began with some governors, has spread to most states, and in the 1996 presidential campaign President Clinton said he would seek funding for 3,000 more charter schools. If charter schools are a radical departure from and a challenge to the existing system, it has the support of very important people in our political system.

Because charter schools are so new—many of them in the planning phase or in operation for a year or so—it may seem premature to examine the concept and what I have learned about these very new schools, especially because I knew that some of what I have to say and predict fits in the category of good news-bad news. I wholeheartedly agree with the concept of charter schools; I predict that their implementation will be self-defeating for most of them. My prediction derives from my 1972 book, *The Creation of Settings and the Future Societies*, in which the complexity of creating a new setting is discussed in detail. For reasons which will be clear in the present book, a critical scrutiny of charter schools, far from being premature, I regard as timely. The reader will, of course, be the final judge.

My friend and educator, Robert Echter, was very helpful to me at certain points in the writing of this book. Dr. Dennis Littky and his cohorts gave me valuable time and opportunity to learn about the new high school they had just opened in Providence, Rhode Island. Abby Weiss of the Institute for Responsive Education at Northeastern University in Boston provided me with the report of her initial study of charter schools and gave me permission to quote extensively from it. I am also indebted to several people who related what they were experiencing in creating a charter school but who preferred anonymity; what they told me in no way conflicts with but rather adds to what Abby Weiss reports. I have studiously avoided reporting anything I have heard in the rumor mill about the difficulties the creators of some charter schools were having, difficulties I concluded in the 1972 book were predictable if and when the creators of new settings were conceptually unprepared for what they had undertaken. And, I can assure the reader, that I know that one is far more likely to learn about difficulties and failures than about instances of smoother sailing. But if anything is disturbing to me, it is that those who in our political arena have initiated and supported the charter school movement have provided no means by which we will ever be able to determine why a charter school succeeded, fell short of its mark, or failed.

Dr. David Blumenkrantz, who is a consultant to several charter schools, provided me with his observations for which I am very appreciative.

As always, in so many small and large ways Lisa Pagliaro—who is as pretty as she is smart and gracious—did not complain about my handwriting, my numerous phone calls to her, or my requests that what I give her today I would like as soon as possible, like yesterday. What I have just said is my way of thanking God for very big favors.

Charter Schools: Another Flawed Educational Reform?

CHAPTER 1

Background and Plan of the Book

I was, of course, gratified at the critical reception of my 1972 book, *The Creation of Settings and the Future Societies*, and very surprised that it was reprinted six times. But I was disappointed that there were no subsequent published accounts containing the kind of detailed, longitudinal description and analysis which would enlarge or require me to change in some way what I had written. When I wrote the book, I was more than a little anxious that I had so little to go on (except for very personal experience in creating the Yale Psycho-Educational Clinic) to develop a conceptual rationale for the creation of settings. I say rationale rather than theory because I wanted to be as concrete as possible. At least as I view theory, it is primarily a set of interrelated abstractions or generalizations intended to explain complicated phenomena, and to do this in as parsimonious a fashion as possible.

I wanted to stay on the level of description so as to enable others to determine from their experience whether some or all of what I would describe rang true. Did the story I would tell—and describing a new setting is a story—make sense? Was I justified in saying that the creation of settings involves processes that will be found in settings which on the surface appear to be in different realms of human activity? This last question was for me the significant one because I had long been critical of the tendency to assume that individuals, groups, and institutions to whom we append different labels have little or no commonalities. I began my professional career in 1942 as a psychologist in a new state institution for mentally retarded individuals, and I spent the next 2 years unlearning all the implications of the labels I had been taught to apply to them. Similarly, when I left that institution to come to Yale where my research brought me into scores of public schools, I accepted the conventional wisdom that schools were unique institutions, an assertion that school personnel considered a glimpse of the obvious. But when I talked with colleagues whose special interest was behavior in diverse types of organizations, and I began seriously to read in that field, I was forced to a conclusion that today is obvious: Schools are not a unique but a different kind of organization. And if I had any doubts on that score, they were quickly dispelled by my observations of how schools reacted to the pressure to change.

It is an instructive experience carefully and slowly to reread a book you wrote a quarter of a century ago. Like it or not, you are reminded that you wrote it at a particular point in your life and in a society that has mightily changed. In an abstract, decontextualized way you already knew that, but rereading puts flesh on the bones of abstraction, and as a consequence, you see yourself and the world in a somewhat different light. What rereading the book forced me to confront was this question: Why could I not cite one published example where what I had written was taken seriously in action? In saying that I leave aside three published accounts which derived from the years of existence of the Yale Psycho-Educational Clinic, during which the creation of settings was an organizing concept for discussion and action. Since that book was written, I have received at least a dozen thick manuscripts describing efforts to create new settings, all of which were partial or total failures. In each case the manuscript was sent to me *after* their effort and as a way of telling me that what I had written clarified why their effort fell so short of the mark. And, again in each instance, they were unsuccessful in getting their manuscript published.

It is not difficult to understand why a publisher would not look kindly at such manuscripts. For one thing, they are long; to describe the creation of a setting and for even one year thereafter is truly a long story. Second, publishers are gun-shy of publishing accounts of failures which, however interesting and of theoretical importance, are not pleasurable to read. Third, the account is about one effort in one site, an institutional case history which, it could be argued, is just that: the single case in which it is hard to determine whether grounds exist to claim generalizability, a claim for which comparable cases hardly exist. Others, as I do, may make the case that creating a new setting is a very frequent occurrence and involves features, processes, and dynamics identical with other instances which on the surface appear to be in very different arenas of human activity and relationships. That argument may be true, but if there is no descriptive literature to indicate that it is true, the single case tends to be viewed as unique, i.e., of no general import. It is a catch-22 situation: First prove that it is generally true despite these surface differences, and then we can determine the significance of the single case you describe at great length.

It is, I trust, understandable from the above why charter schools are of great significance to me. After all, they are by explicit design new settings intended to demonstrate innovative ideas which if their creators have unusual freedom will not only inform the mission and organization of the school but will bring about better, more superior outcomes. That I would look very favorably on the concept of charter schools was quite predictable from my diverse critiques of our schools (Sarason, 1990, 1993a–c,

1995). However, if I considered the concept of a charter school refresh-ing, necessary, and potentially extraordinarily instructive, I confess that I had very strong misgivings that their potentials would be realized. For one thing, I realistically assumed that those who led the charter school move-ment, who lobbied for the legislation creating charter schools, who had the responsibility to select the schools, and who created and ran these schools had never read my book. That, I hasten to add, is not the com-plaint of an author who thinks he has said the last word about the cre-ation of settings and is disappointed that after publishing his thoughts the world goes on its less-than-merry way, unaware of what he has written. I may have harbored such hopes and fantasies 57 years ago when I wrote my first paper, but it did not take long for that hope to extinguish and to be content with experiencing, thinking, and writing. That there were in-dividuals who responded positively to my writings was, as it always is, heartwarming, even though on an institutional level nothing changed.

If I knew I had not said the last word on the creation of settings, I knew I was one who probably had said an early word, which is why I had such anxiety in writing the book. There is a large literature on new set-tings, ranging over time from accounts of the communes in the nineteenth century to those in the 1960s and 1970s of the present century. Communes were but one type of new setting described in the literature. The fact is that all of these instances were retrospective accounts written very long after the setting had been conceived and organized, when the vicissitudes of memory had done their work and the details of the before-the-beginning phase were impossible to determine. (I say that because, as the present book emphasizes: The degree of success or failure of a new setting is largely determined by its prehistory and what happened in its first operational year.) Despite its shortcomings there was enough in the available litera-ture to justify my attempt to try to conceptualize what goes into the cre-ation of a new setting. Activists, and that is what creators of settings are, tend not to be readers. (But, then again, readers tend not to be activists.) Matters are not helped any by the challenge of the vision and then of the opportunity to bring the vision to life, a challenge so alluring and moti-vating, so focussed on the distinctive ideas to be built into the setting, as to make reading of the past efforts of others seem unnecessary. New set-tings have the imprint of the dynamics of the myth of uniqueness.

When I became aware early in the 1990s that some states had passed enabling legislation to create charter schools, I began to think about the kind of charter school I would seek to create and why, assuming of course that I was younger than I was, much younger. It was the "why" that in-trigued me because I had concluded that schools would not improve unless and until the difference between contexts of productive and unproduc-tive learning were recognized and taken seriously. That had led me to write

How Schools Might Be Governed and Why (1997). The more I thought about charter schools, the more I was persuaded that I would have next to write the present book. I started to talk with some individuals who were going to seek to create a charter school, and I also talked with some who were already in the pre-operational or before-the-beginning phase. It was apparent to me that creators of settings were conceptually unprepared for what they would predictably encounter. If they did not regard creating a setting as merely a kind of engineering or logistical process, they certainly had no conception of the complexity ahead. I secured from several state departments of education the administrative guidelines describing the criteria by which applications to create a charter school would be judged. But I also read them to determine whether those state guidelines recognized in any way the complexity of creating a setting. After all, if you are going to select among applications, should not your stated criteria at least suggest that an applicant have some sensitivity to how predictable problems will be dealt with, that precisely because it is a new setting one has to expect that some problems have a high probability of occurrence? I learned what I expected: nothing, unless absence of what you wanted to read is something

There was another "nothing," a very predictable one. Should not an innovation, a radical departure from tradition—one requiring special legislation—be carefully described and assessed, not only to determine degree of success or failure, but to have a basis for learning how future charter schools might better be planned for? If Model A has flaws, how do we correct for them in Model B? For all practical purposes the state legislation provides no meaningful support for the purposes of learning how to improve Model A. And I say the same for a current federal effort at assessment, a superficial effort either because the assessors have little or no understanding of the creation of settings or the funds available for the effort compromised the scope and depth of what should be done, all of this at the same time that the federal government seeks to support the creation of 3,000 more charter schools. It is not the first time that state and federal governments plunge ahead as if where and how they have started will *of course* not require rethinking and revision. I do not regard charter schools as kin to so many educational fads and fashions that have had their 15 minutes of celebrity and then deservedly disappeared. Unlike most of those fads and fashions of the past, charter schools legislation was enacted because of initiatives and support of some state governors who knew that the past failures of reform efforts said a great deal about existing school systems and their intractability to those efforts (Sarason, 1990). As I expected, political leaders are quite adept at directing blame to groups and forces outside the political system. Implicitly and explicitly these political leaders saw past reform failures as indicative of an educational system incapable of reforming itself. If I agreed with them on that point, I very much disagreed with the way they saw themselves as having played no role in those failures. They had learned nothing. They talked about charter schools as if creating them would not be beset with problems. Indeed, I never heard any of these political leaders say anything to suggest that there would or might be problems which would be a basis for learning how future charter schools could avoid those problems. It was as if there was nothing to learn about charter schools. Why spend money to study them when it was obvious that the concept of charter schools made so much sense? The result is that we will never know why some charter schools were successful and, as I reluctantly predict, many more will be unsuccessful. I discuss these issues of political influence in regard to charter schools and more in my most recent book, *Political Leadership and Educational Failure* (1998).

Charter schools have to be seen in a historical perspective in order to gain some sense of the nature of the social pressures to produce an educational system maximizing uniformity of purpose and practice, a uniformity challenged by the nature of charter schools which are encouraged and allowed to depart from a stifling uniformity. In addition to a brief historical overview, Chapter 2 describes the fate and significance of a precursor of charter schools: President Nixon's well-funded Experimental Schools Program.

Chapter 3 is devoted to those experiences in my professional career, beginning in 1942, which led me to create the Yale Psycho-Educational Clinic in 1961–62 and then to write the 1972 book. Each of those experiences contributed in an unplanned way to the realization that the process and dynamics of creating a setting required description, analysis, and conceptualization. Although that book contains some material directly relevant to schools, my major purpose was to indicate that the creation of settings was a process and problem that went far beyond the educational arena. After that book was published, I regretted that I did not include more about schools. Charter schools were not then on the horizon, but if they were, it would have made writing the book easier than it was. (More correctly, less difficult than it was.)

It is in Chapter 4 that I present and discuss the most essential features and problems of the process whereby new settings come into existence and the predictable problems they will confront. I know of no instance where those problems were avoided, and I know of no instance where the creators were at all conceptually prepared for what was ahead and took preventive steps to dilute their thorniness. I am confident that the reader will agree that these predictable features are no arcane mystery. If they are predictable, they are also understandable. The fact is, I argue, that the creation of a setting, precisely because of the creator's sense of innovative mission, triggers complicated interpersonal dynamics, an unrealistic time perspective, the "happy family" syndrome, and an insensitivity to the external surround in which some individuals and agencies see the new setting in negative terms. Since it is very rare that those who create the setting have previously engaged in the process, and they lack a conceptual road map, what gets triggered can be quite disruptive. And, I emphasize in that chapter, not everyone who wants to create a new setting has the temperament and skills to deal adequately with those problems.

Readers may be surprised that Chapter 5 is not about charter schools but about a willing merger of two organizations who seek to create a new setting which will be better and stronger than each is alone, and insure that the merged setting will more than merely survive in a fiercely competitive world. That is to say, the mission of the merged setting is to allow each of the parties to achieve its distinctive goals. Aside from the fact that I wanted to remind the reader that creating a new setting takes place in very different arenas of society, the two mergers I discuss illustrate the difference between leadership that is realistic about predictable problems, and leadership that assumes that good will and strong motivation will be sufficient to overcome whatever problems will be encountered.

Chapter 6 looks at charter schools in terms of the features common to the process of creating a setting. Helpful in this respect was the publication of a study (Weiss, 1997) of five charter schools in Massachusetts which had been in existence for one year. Although each school was visited for only one day, I was very surprised how what I described and predicted was evident. It is likely to be the case that, as in the Massachusetts report, descriptive evaluation studies will totally ignore the before-the-beginning phase which is so crucial in the fate of the setting. I should tell the reader that I have been told about charter schools which either never became operational or are having a very stormy time. I have heard little about charter schools who are developing as hoped; those kinds of settings tend not to become grist for the rumor mill. Whether what I predict holds up well, of course, cannot be determined unless future studies do justice to the complexity of the process of creating a setting. That is why I am so critical of political leaders who in regard to innovations in education do not do what they insist on in regard to other social problems: to carefully and dispassionately study the innovation before replicating it in large numbers.

Chapter 7 examines charter schools in light of what we know about a new setting that is the most comprehensively described (and successful) instance I have found: The creation by the Manhattan Project during World

War II of the Los Alamos setting to determine if an atomic bomb could be developed before Germany did. However one regards atomic energy or bombs, Los Alamos is extraordinarily relevant to the conceptualization of the creation of settings. The Los Alamos story is complex, but I have concentrated on those features most relevant to elaborate in that chapter on the implementation of the concept of charter schools.

I defined a new setting as when two or more people get together over a sustained period of time to achieve agreed-upon goals. I recognized in the 1972 book that "two or more" and "agreed-upon goals" represent ambiguities. The more I investigated charter schools as concept and process the more I felt it important further to discuss the two ambiguities, which I do in Chapter 8. By their very mission charter schools have numerous stakeholders who are to have a role, a leadership role, in creating the setting. There may be one or two people who for purposes of applying for charter school status are designated "leaders," but informally there is agreement that all major stakeholders are part of the leadership team. States usually require that there be the equivalent of a board of trustees, and those stakeholders are represented there, although they may participate more intimately in all that goes on in the planning process and after the settling becomes operational. In the charter schools I know most about, there are, appearances aside, more than one leader. That, of course, can be a source of problems, especially if the fantasy that "everyone will pull together" and "everybody is in full agreement about goals" is strong. That is the fantasy which permits people to confuse what is depicted on an organizational chart with the realities of the organization (Sarason & Lorentz, 1997). To illustrate what can and does frequently happen, Chapter 8 contains a more detailed account of three new settings in which I have worked. They are briefly mentioned in Chapter 3 but described in more detail in Chapter 8. Precisely because charter schools have at least several stakeholders from its earliest beginnings, the relevance of the contents of this chapter have to be taken into account if we are ever to have an understanding of the degree of success and failures of these schools.

Chapter 9 is about a new and non-traditional high school in Providence, Rhode Island. I am writing about it after its first year of operation. Although it is not designated as a charter, it has all of the intended features of a charter school. Thus far it appears to be devoid of the worst consequences that so often mark a new setting, and I give my explanation of what appears to be a setting moving well to meeting its purposes.

In Chapter 10 I briefly discuss those features of creating settings I consider bedrock in determining the fate of the new setting.

In writing this book I tried hard to avoid mentioning things told to me in private conversations which may or may not have been true; I simply had no basis for generalizing from their anecdotes and opinions, even though most of what was told to me confirmed my fears about the fate of most charter schools. But after this book was finished and sent off to the publisher in late 1997, news articles, troubling ones, about charter schools began to appear in the *New York Times* and some Arizona dailies (I visit Arizona twice a year). Those news articles I regard as "signals." It is highly likely that similar news articles have appeared in other newspapers in other states. I decided, therefore, to add Chapter 11 to this book.

I have to reiterate that this book was not written because sufficient data permitting conclusions are available. But my understanding and description of the creation of settings was based on enough instances from different arenas to write the 1972 book. Nothing since its publication has caused me to change what I wrote. So, when charter schools came on the scene, and I began to learn what I could about those being planned and those who are past that stage, I felt both justified and compelled to write the present book.

CHAPTER 2

A Historical Perspective on Charter Schools

Several developments historically contributed to schools as we know them today. Each in its own way concerned the nature and limits of the state to make policies for and oversee the educational system. Today's charter school movement, far from challenging state power and responsibility, is testimony to the state's power to exempt a public school from the obligation to be bound by burdensome and confining state regulations that are obstacles to the achievement of its educational goals. Understandably, charter schools are seen as a challenge to and a devastating critique of existing school systems, and it is fair to say that critique derived in large measure from the perception that schools in our metropolitan areas—comprised as they are of poor, very diverse minority, immigrant, linguistic, religious groups—were educationally inferior and a source of social divisiveness. Although I say "in large measure," I must add that the critique is embedded in a general dissatisfaction with the performance of American public schools. Charter schools are seen by its proponents as a step to a radical overhaul of American public education. A majority of states have some form of charter school legislation, and my home state of Connecticut is not alone in adopting the policy that a significant number of charter schools should be in the state's urban areas.

What I find interesting about the charter school movement is that historically the conditions to which it is a response were created by the state's goal to provide a mandated *uniform* education for *all* children regardless of their cultural, social class, or religious background. And in contrast to charter school ideology, that goal totally ignored anything resembling a formal role for parents in matters educational. Wave after wave of immigration, the increasing bureaucratization of the school system, and the professionalization of teaching produced a structure and purpose of which schools today are the lineal descendants, and that is also the case in regard to the substance of the controversies in and around schools. Today's schools were not born yesterday. The social conflicts surrounding legislation for compulsory education are still with us today. That, as we shall now see, should occasion surprise only in those people who, like Henry Ford, see "history as bunk." In the paragraphs that follow, those who read today's mass media will recognize themes that different groups in different parts of the country articulate.

In Tyack's (1976) analysis of the history of compulsory education in the United States he distinguishes two phases. The first was from 1852, when Massachusetts adopted its compulsory-attendance law, to about 1890, when most states adopted compulsory-attendance legislation which was generally unenforced if not unenforceable. This stage, which he calls *symbolic*, was characterized by ideological dispute rather than practical implementation. The second phase, designated the *bureaucratic* phase, began shortly before the turn of the century. It was a time in which American school systems grew in size and complexity, techniques of bureaucratic control evolved, compulsory schooling laws were strengthened, and enforcement was increasingly effective.

In the 1890s, the right of the state to enforce compulsory education was still under challenge, primarily a Catholic challenge. One of the most important of these challenges and one which attracted much national attention was to occur in relation to the Ohio compulsory education law of 1879. Father Quigley, pastor of a Catholic school in Toledo, chose on constitutional grounds not to comply with that section of the law which required him to make quarterly reports to the state. He was arrested and brought to trial and convicted. The Court found in favor of the state (Burns, 1969).

Tyack is probably right in stating that, during the second phase of bureaucratic compulsory education, ideological conflict over compulsory attendance diminished. But other aspects of the state's right to control education did continue to provoke ideological conflict, particularly in the area of state control over private and parochial schools, and these conflicts were at times intertwined with the compulsory attendance issue. For if the state could require compulsory school attendance—and even Catholics following the court rulings of the 1890s, reluctantly or not, had to grant that—did that not also imply that the state might determine the kind of school and the nature of the instruction that would fulfill the compulsory attendance requirement?

These further encroachments of the state on the rights of the family, church, and ethnic groups were to coincide with yet another periodic upheaval of nativist sentiment that developed about the time of World War I. From the year 1905, when the annual immigration first exceeded the one million mark, through 1914, approximately 10,000,000 immigrants came to the United States. Increasingly after the turn of the century this immigration had become dominated by eastern and southern European national groups. In addition to the social concerns such large numbers of immigrants might reasonably evoke, there was much alarm in nativist circles—reinforced by the developing eugenics movement—that this influx of inferior blood would dilute, if not wash away in a flood, the superior Nordic blood of the founding fathers.

If the outbreak of World War I gave some temporary relief by drastically reducing the number of new immigrants, it also made the nativists more concerned about the loyalty of the foreigners already in their midst. As a result, there developed simultaneously a clamor for restrictive immigration laws and a vigorous program for Americanizing the immigrant. To the public schools, naturally, was assigned a major role in this Americanizing program. Grade school and high school programs increasingly emphasized the cultivation of patriotism and good citizenship and even became involved in adult education programs for the immigrant (Atzmon, 1958; Thompson, 1971). What is of particular interest to us in this Americanization program is the fact that by 1919, some 16 states had passed laws prohibiting the teaching of foreign languages in all public *and* private primary schools (O'Brien, 1961).

The crucial legal test of these laws began in Nebraska when Robert Meyer, a teacher in a parochial school sponsored by the Zion Evangelical Lutheran Church, was convicted of having taught a 10-year-old child to read in German through the use of Bible stories. In reversing Meyer's conviction in 1923, the U.S. Supreme Court based itself on the clause of the Fourteenth Amendment which holds that a state may not deprive an individual of "life, liberty, or property, without the due process of law." In explicating the word *liberty*, the Court held that it included not merely freedom from bodily restraint but the right "to enjoy those privileges long recognized at common law as essential to the orderly pursuit of happiness by free men." Within this construction the court held that the rights of Meyer to teach the German language as part of his occupation and the rights of the parents to engage him to so instruct their children had been violated by the state. The Court took this position while it explicitly indicated it did not intend to question the power of the state "to compel attendance at some school and to make reasonable regulations for all schools" (Stakes & Pfeffer, 1950, p. 737). The Court was recognizing the need for balancing the rights of individual, family, and state. But in the spirit of the times, attempted encroachment by the state on individual, family, and church rights continued.

In 1920, the Scottish Rite Masons, Southern Jurisdiction of the United States, publicly proclaimed their belief that the only sure foundation of our free institutions was the education of all children in public primary schools in which instruction should be restricted to the English language (Tyack, 1968). With Scottish Rite support, a proposed amendment to the

Michigan constitution requiring public school attendance for all students was advanced in the same year but soundly defeated in referendum (Holsinger, 1968). The scene of activity in this campaign to destroy the parochial schools then shifted to the Northwest where, with Masonic support and vigorous backing by the Ku Klux Klan, Oregon voters exercised that favorite democratic device of the progressive era, the initiative, to pass a law in 1922 essentially requiring all children between the ages of 8 and 16 to attend public schools. Penalties of fines and imprisonment were to be imposed on parents who failed to comply. Sponsors of the law had aimed it specifically at the Catholic school system, but with populist and patriotic fervor they extended their rhetoric to the snobbish private schools of the blue bloods and those private schools which were designated to further the cause of Bolshevism (Holsinger, 1968; Tyack, 1968).

Prior to the projected date of implementation of the law, the Society of Sisters of the Holy Names of Jesus and Mary, which operated a parochial school, and the Hill Military Academy sought a court injunction. Before the U.S. District Court, counsel for the Sisters argued that the law would, among other things, deprive the society of property without due process of law and deprive the parents of the right to control the education of their children. The state argued that increased attendance at nonpublic schools had been accompanied by an increase in juvenile delinquency and that compulsory attendance at public schools was necessary as a "precautionary measure against the moral pestilence of paupers, vagabonds, and possibly convicts" and that children educated in nonpublic schools would be exposed to the doctrines of "Bolshevists, syndicalists, and communists" (Jorgenson, 1968, p. 462). Further, if any one denomination were permitted to conduct schools, others would do so and that would lead to the destruction of the public school system. The state therefore freely admitted that the intent of the law was to destroy nonpublic schools. "The necessity for any other kind of school than that provided by the State has ceased to exist" (Jorgenson, 1968, p. 462).

The District Court issued an injunction restraining the state from putting the law into effect. The state appealed to the Supreme Court. Meanwhile, the excesses of nativism and nationalism of the World War period began to subside; immigration was well below the pre-War levels and the Ku Klux Klan mentality was beginning to recede. On the whole, the national press was vigorous in its denunciation of the Oregon law and the court challenges of the Sisters were vigorously supported by Protestant and Jewish groups.

Uniformity of curriculum and school organization, fears of the consequences of immigrant groups from all over the world, controversy about bilingual programs, by whom and how should power over educational policy be wielded, which rituals of a patriotic or religious significance (saluting the flag, saying the Lord's Prayer) should be mandatory in school, to what extent and how the curriculum should portray the roles of diverse racial and racial groups—these issues go back a long way in the history of American public schools. And, it needs to be emphasized, the rise of parochial schools (Catholic, Protestant, and Jewish) was an explicit reaction to the perception and reality of state power to have a uniform school system which, to say the least, was not hospitable to diversity of views and practices. That is why the recent appearance and growing momentum of the charter school movement is so interesting: The states are both encouraging and legislatively supporting the creation of schools to go their own way, to depart from the rules and regulations making for uniformity. States vary in the scope and freedom given to their charter schools, but all states in principle agree that these schools should be free radically to depart from rules and regulations of all other schools.

A second development relevant to my purposes was the 1954 desegregation decision. At the same time the decision rendered unconstitutional an earlier court decision that had justified "separate but equal" school systems, one for whites and one for blacks, the 1954 decision essentially said that the state had an obligation to bring about an integrated and uniform school system with "all deliberate speed." I need not describe the turmoil, controversy, and open conflict that followed efforts to implement the decision. At the time no one would have predicted that four decades later some black leaders and educators would call for all black schools (in Milwaukee and Boston), some for boys and some for girls. Such proposals went nowhere because they were considered unconstitutional in a basic sense and in violation of civil rights legislation. But the proponents had made an important point: Psychologically and educationally the public schools were inimical to the needs and values of black youth, a position that had been taken in earlier times by other groups faced with state power, rules, and regulations that made for a uniformity insensitive to their culture and background. It is no surprise, therefore, that state legislation for the creating charter schools has given rise to a policy that requires that a significant number of these schools should be in urban areas where blacks and other minorities predominate. That is not to suggest that the stimulus for charter schools was a result of the racial and ethnic issues or even of the ever–widening gulf in educational and vocational outcomes of students in urban and suburban schools. That gulf was but one factor contributing to a more general view that American school systems had been intractable to reform efforts and a different and more radical approach was necessary. And that conclusion about schools in general rested on the diagnosis that the culture of schools bulwarked perspectives and an entrenched bureaucratic structure which sustained a self-defeating uniformity at the expense of any meaningful innovation. It is that diagnosis which gave rise to the charter school movement, and if it was a diagnosis about schools in general, it was predictable that enabling state legislation would be seen as having special salience for urban areas and their ineffective schools.

Because history is so frequently seen as a museum of relics and facts only to be visited on weekends or rainy days, I must call attention to a federal precursor of charter schools. This was President Nixon's Experimental Schools Program (ESP) which encouraged, selected, and supported schools to refashion themselves and essentially to create a new setting with relative freedom from past constraints, federal and local. No less than in the case of charter schools, the ESP was proclaimed as the wave of the future, as a kind of unleashing of the creativity and energies of parents, students, and educators, as a delegation of unprecedented authority to implement a new vision.

That program not only had the support of the president but also that of the president's Science Advisory Committee and the top officials in the Department of Health, Education, and Welfare. The ESP was based explicitly on a recognition of the inadequacies of past efforts, a recognition that was as refreshing as it was singular. Very briefly, the ESP rested on several considerations:

- Past federal efforts to improve and change schools were largely failures.
- Federal programs had a buckshot quality: there was a program for this part of the school system and for that one; there was a program for this educational problem and for that one. It was as if the federal government kept reacting to whatever problem was brought to its attention. Sequence and interconnectedness were not important.
- The federal government should provide the resources for *comprehensive* change in a school system; that is, sufficient resources to permit a school district more meaningfully and efficiently "to put it all together" in a single direction.
- There was merit in the complaints of local districts that federal imposition of programs, or too many intrusions by federal personnel into planning at the local level, robbed local people of initiative, creativity, and control. In the ESP local people would have more control over ESP projects. If local districts were sincerely given the opportunity to change their schools in ways they considered most appropriate, one could then count on their commitment to initiate and sustain the change process.
- Federal efforts to evaluate past reform efforts had been inadequate, and they bore no relationship either to changes in federal policy or to local

program management. The ESP would use innovative and rigorous social science methodology to understand and assess the change process better. Indeed, somewhat less than one-third of the $60–70 million that the ESP would cost would go to an evaluation scheme no less comprehensive than the changes that local districts would bring about in their schools.

The ESP was a disaster and anyone who has any doubts on that score should read Cowden and Cohen's (n.d.) federally sponsored assessment.

Most assuredly, I gain no satisfaction from having predicted the failure of the ESP, but one had to be inordinately obtuse not to have made such a prediction. Somewhere near the point when the policymakers were to decide which school districts would be part of the ESP, I was asked to come to Washington to advise on these decisions. It was a chaotic visit on several scores. Federal personnel felt tremendous pressure to launch this well-publicized program as soon as possible, preferably yesterday. I could not decide whether the pressure was more internal or external, although as the meeting wore on the internal drive seemed to be the major source. That feeling of pressure seemed very much related to the federal personnel's vast underestimation of how much time it would take to select approximately 20 school districts. Because the local districts would have the most to say about how they would bring about comprehensive change, that kind of freedom made the task of selection very difficult. How does one choose on the basis of a written grant request (and telephone calls) except by resorting to one's own conception about how comprehensive change *should* be accomplished? That issue came quickly to the fore when one perused the written documents at different stages of their submission; they were vague statements of virtuous intent, giving one no sense of security about how "comprehensive change" was being defined. However committed federal personnel had been to the idea of local initiative and control, that commitment quickly began to dissolve as they concluded that local districts were defining comprehensive change in strange and various ways. The written documents were more like inkblots, forcing the reader to intuit what local districts meant by what they said and wrote. The truth is that the local districts were as much at sea about the meaning of "comprehensive change" as the federal personnel were.

My second contact with the ESP was a year later when I was asked to assess the plans and resources of a private consulting firm seeking the contract for the first in a series of evaluation studies. By this time most of the local districts to be part of the ESP had been chosen and their final grant applications were made available to us. Each application was no less than 4 inches thick and weighed 5 or more pounds. Their bulk was matched only by their lack of substance. That may sound like an excessively harsh judgment, but no one at this second meeting came to a contrary conclusion; it was obvious to everyone that these applications presented no focus to evaluate—no conceptual or procedural framework. It was painful to observe the staff of the consulting firm, a methodologically sophisticated group, trying to reconcile their desire to get the contract with the inkblot character of what they were supposed to do. The federal staff wanted a rigorous evaluation, but they had maneuvered themselves into a classically tragic situation in which the beginnings already contained the seeds of everyone's ultimate defeat. This judgment is well documented by Cowden and Cohen (n.d.) and will not be further discussed here.

I have not related this and other experiences merely to indicate that initiating, managing, and sustaining "comprehensive" change involving schools and community agencies are complex affairs. Nor is it my intention to add to the collection of horror stories. My use of these instances is the basis they provide to make several points. The first is that any effort at primary prevention in schools, geared as it almost always is, to the prevention of student problems, cannot ignore the necessity for the adults (professional or lay) who will implement the effort to change in ways consistent with that effort. Put another way, the effort always will require that these people literally *reform* their attitudes and practices. To put it more baldly: these people have to be seen initially as part of the problem, not as tailor-made for the solution. I am in no way suggesting that they should be viewed as clinical specimens possessing characteristics absent in "us." Like us, they come to the effort with attitudes and practices that contributed to the need for the new effort. To ignore this point, to proceed as if verbal agreement and commitment are sufficient for change, is defeating of one's goals.

This is why I said earlier that proclaiming adherence to the goals of primary prevention is not inherently virtuous. To achieve these goals requires processes and a long-term time perspective too frequently overlooked or egregiously oversimplified, which is another way of saying that your conception of the particular conditions you seek to prevent was woefully incomplete. The goals of primary prevention rest on some understanding of the factors contributing to the conditions you seek to prevent. In the case of our schools those conditions are *in part* always a reflection of the attitudes and practices of those who participate in the new effort.

The second, obviously related to the first, is that the goals of primary prevention are achievable only if the dynamics of secondary prevention have been successfully overcome. If those participating in the effort are *part* of the problem, how can you dilute the adverse consequences of their overlearned attitudes and practices? To get to the point where primary prevention becomes a possibility, you must have successfully confronted and overcome the consequences of these past attitudes and practices.

The third point is less obvious than the first two. Is it not a fateful mistake to formulate the goals of primary prevention *only* in terms of what you want to prevent in pupils? If it is indeed true that educational personnel are part of the problem, should we not be paying more attention to how we might select and prepare these personnel so that they will be less of a problem than they are now?

I should hasten to add that I did not bring up the ESP as a basis for predicting that charter schools will also be a total disaster. In later chapters I will state my reservations about what charter schools will demonstrate and accomplish. As I indicate in my 1997 book, *How Schools Might Be Governed and Why,* it is clear that I am a proponent of the *concept* of the charter school. But as later chapters will indicate, there is a minefield of obstacles between concept and achievement of goals consistent with that concept, and those obstacles are identical to those on which the ESP foundered; with one exception: the ESP schools were well funded, charter schools receive approximately the same amount for each pupil as would have been given for that student in a traditional school. Precisely because charter schools traverse uncharted seas it would not be unreasonable or an instance of fiscal imprudence for charter schools to be able to request some additional funds, but policy makers are notoriously risk aversive to a self-defeating degree. More of this later.

Charter schools have to be seen in relation to several features of the post-World War II school reform effort.

1. Billions upon billions of dollars have been spent to change and improve schools with consequences the opposite of robust.
2. There is a classroom here and a classroom there, a school here and a school there, where an effort at reform has been successful. *Those efforts do not spread or diffuse; they remain isolated, uninfluential efforts.*
3. As students go from the elementary to the middle to the high school, their motivation for learning decreases as does their disinterest in subject matter, and their boredom increases.
4. When people, knowledgeable people, are asked "If you were starting from scratch, would you come up with the educational system we have today?" no one answers in the affirmative. Few are able to suggest even in outline what system they would substitute, but all perceive the present system as a seriously flawed one.

The purpose of this chapter was to indicate why I regard charter schools as of the greatest theoretical and practical significance. For one thing, charter schools rest on a devastating critique of the present system because it implies that for a school meaningfully to innovate to achieve more desirable outcomes, it must be free of the usual rules, regulations, and traditions of a school system. That conclusion is an *implicit* one; it has never been made explicit by proponents of charter schools who usually assert that these schools will contribute to the improvement of schools generally. What those contributions may be, and why and how they will exert an influence has never been made clear. Several questions have to be asked. Will the present system truly permit and support charter schools? Will the system, formally or informally, be an obstacle to charter schools? Will charter schools be assessed in ways permitting us to determine why this charter school succeeded and that one failed? On the basis of what we know about the creation of new settings, what predictions can be made about the number that will succeed or fail are warranted? Granted that charter schools are in their early phases, on the basis of what we know about them, do they confirm or disconfirm what we know about the creation of settings? Before we can begin to address these questions, it is necessary that the next chapter be devoted to the origins of the conceptualization about why and how new settings arise and so many of them fail at achieving their purposes.

CHAPTER 3

Some Personal Experiences

In the 1972 book I defined a new setting as one in which two or more people get together in new and sustained relationships to achieve agreed-upon goals. Marriage, legal or not, is the smallest instance, and national revolution, the most ambitious; in between those extremes is an array of instances which on the surface are bewilderingly heterogeneous, so much so as to call into question the heuristic value of the definition. Let me very briefly describe in chronological order the experiences, events, and observations that led me (after more than three decades) to formulate and describe commonalities in the creation of settings despite their obvious surface differences.

1. My first professional job was in a newly opened state institution for mentally retarded individuals in Connecticut. In terms of its architecture, layout, and educational rationale, the Southbury Training School was literally unique and revolutionary. By the time I left in 1945, after more than 3 years living and working there, I had to conclude that Southbury had not and would not achieve its goals, a conclusion that its subsequent history amply confirmed (including being put under the jurisdiction of the courts). It is a very complex story (on which I expand in Chapter 8), but by the time I left several things seemed to me part of the explanation. First, even before Southbury opened its door there had been power struggles in state officialdom about who should be its first superintendent and what the relationship should be with the other, far-older comparable state institution. These controversies led to compromises that were inimical to its educational goals. Second, the first superintendent, whose personal virtues were many and unassailable, knew next to nothing about mental retardation. Below him were directors of several large departments: medical, residential living, education and training, social service, business-accounting, plant maintenance. Although each department was autonomous and its director "formally" of equal status and power to other directors, it was obvious to everyone that the superintendent depended for direction and advice on only one director. To say that there were power struggles among the directors, that the level of animosity among them was high is to indulge understatement. The rumor mill operated 24 hours a day, centering around two questions: How

Southbury "really" should be governed and by whom? Third, and for me was most puzzling, was that among the directors there was surprising little agreement about Southbury's mission and goals, even though Southbury's refreshingly radical mission and goals were the reasons these individuals (and many more) sought positions there. Fourth, the great bulk of employees—those in direct contact with the residents—resented and hostilely resigned themselves to the obvious fact that "those on top" could not care less about their problems, daily experience, ideas, and advice. They felt frustrated, voiceless, unrecognized, and unimportant.

   2. In 1945 I came to Yale's Institute of Human Relations (IHR) in which the department of psychology was then housed. IHR had been created 15 years earlier with much fanfare because it was the first and most ambitious effort by an American university to bring together the social sciences with the goal of integrating them, of forging a truly interdisciplinary working ambience in which a synthesis (theoretical, methodological, and practical) of what was best in these disciplines would emerge. IHR was not a department but a large, impressive building housing eminent representatives of the social sciences who would have more than adequate physical and financial resources provided by a large, long-term Rockefeller grant. When I came to Yale, it did not take long for me to conclude that there was little interdisciplinary ferment in IHR. There were fiefdoms, interpersonal animosities, and in one instance bolted doors between one fiefdom and the rest of IHR. IHR had become a paper organization with a budget. Several years after I arrived, IHR went out of existence. From numerous sources I learned several things about its early history. First, the crucial person in IHR's creation was President Angell who was the first Yale president who was not an alumnus, a fact that did not endear him to the Yale faculty. Indeed, powerful forces in the faculty were opposed to the concept of the IHR, an opposition further fueled by the fact that Yale departments are notoriously allergic to any program, institute, and agency not housed in and controlled by a department. In other words, precisely because IHR was explicitly designed to bypass departmental control, it was, so to speak, a sitting duck for at best noncooperation and at worst an object of malign neglect. The combination of presidential power and Rockefeller money carried the day but at a price the creators did not envision. Second, there was much argument about where the new buildings should be. Crucial in that decision was the powerful (and autocratic) dean of the medical school who wanted IHR across the street from the medical school and the New Haven hospital. Whatever the prickly faults of Dean Winternitz, the fact is that he very sincerely believed that the social sciences had much to contribute to the understanding of medical problems. There was, of course, the opposing argument that by its very mission IHR should be

near social science departments and not several blocks away in a slum area. The reality was that the Yale academic community wanted IHR any place but on what is euphemistically called the Yale campus. (Yale was built and developed in and around the Broadway and Forty-Second Street of New Haven.) IHR was built across the street from the hospital, several blocks away in another social, economic, ethnic, racial world. Third, although Yale was very successful in attracting a variety of senior academic "stars" to IHR, it quickly became apparent that these individuals had not become stars by virtue of cooperative endeavors with comparable people in sister disciplines but rather by possessing the characteristics of rugged individualists. Someone said to me that IHR should have been renamed The Institute for Individual Ambition and Achievement. Fourth, the first director of IHR was an unimpressive, decent person with minor academic credentials unaccustomed and unable to deal with, let along lead, academic stars. Fifth, as best as I was able to determine the governance structure was (and remained) a mystery.

3. A couple of years after coming to Yale in 1945 I developed a research project on test anxiety which required that I spend a lot of time in a lot of schools in three Connecticut cities. More correctly, two of the communities were towns which rather quickly became cities as a consequence of the baby and building boom. I observed the building and creation of at least 20 schools. In each instance the new principal saw the new school as an opportunity to innovate in ways that would be better or superior to what he or she had previously experienced; for example, selecting "better" teachers, forging close collegial relationships, integrating the curriculum in productive ways, developing a more knowledgeable and supportive parent constituency, being more responsive to individual needs of students and teachers, and creating a climate in which divisiveness and personal rivalries would be kept to a minimum. It would be fair to say that the principal's vision was one of the happy family in which every member took satisfaction in being part of the family. It was *not* a vision of unconnected individuals. For several reasons that vision was totally undetectable or at best minimally detectable at the end of the first 2 years of the schools. The first reason was that in more than a few of these schools the principal, despite his or her public rhetoric, acted in ways that were subversive of collegiality; decision making was the principal's sole prerogative; teachers saw no point in offering advice, let alone criticism; and faculty meetings were routinized, unstimulating rituals. The style and purposes of governance were not and could not be discussed. Teachers "retreated" to their safe, isolated classrooms. In other new schools principals came to see the school system's administrative hierarchy as placing obstacles to the implementation of the vision, or being unresponsive or unsupportive

or reneging on promises made before the school opened. This view had to be seen in the context of a more general view shared by these new schools: Existing schools in the system were jealous of them (their large, more attractive space as well as what seemed to be a freedom to innovate) and complained that the hierarchy compared existing schools unfavorably to the new ones. In one respect, a most crucial one, in all of these new schools the principal was appointed toward the end of the previous school year; the selection of teachers was (to say the least) a hurried affair; the first time the principal and teachers were in the same room was a few days before the school opened, with the result that for the first few weeks the stresses, frustrations, and anxieties were destabilizing for everyone, none or few of whom had ever been part of creating a new setting. That, in part, explains why some principals felt forced to use power autocratically and other principals put their vision on hold. In any event, by the end of 2 years, and apart from their obvious newness, these schools were not different from the existing ones. This is not to say that by conventional standards they were unacceptable or below par schools but rather that they were not the schools that had been created to be distinctively different from the modal American school.

4. When the federal government passed the Head Start legislation in the mid sixties, it meant that several thousand new settings would be created. I and colleagues at the Yale Psycho-Educational Clinic had the opportunity to observe three such programs before and after they were operational. In the preoperational phase discussion, planning, and semi-explosive controversy centered on several questions. Who should have responsibility and control of the program? Where would or should the program be housed? By what criteria should directors be chosen, and who would make final decisions? What would be the responsibilities and role of parents? Because there would be more children than slots, how would children be selected? How many of the staff should have professional credentials, and by whom and what criteria will aides be selected? It was hard to avoid three conclusions. First, there was a power struggle within the black community about who would control the program. Second, most black participants wanted to prevent domination of the program by white educators; the racial divide was never explicitly discussed, but it was a significant factor. Third, for all practical purposes educational issues were hardly discussed; it was as if there was no need to become explicit about what a stimulating preschool experience should be. If issues of power dominated in the preoperational phase, they continued in a somewhat different form after the programs began. There were conflicts between parents and staff, as there were between teachers and aides, as there were between consultants and staff. Much of what I have

described was known to and predicted by the founders of Head Start who were primarily concerned with the substance of the educational component and the training and quality of staff, concerns which if not addressed they feared would limit the benefits children would derive from these programs. If those concerns were taken seriously, it would have meant that these programs would not have started as quickly as the legislation required, and it would have required additional funds for training and selection purposes. The Head Start programs were conceived, created, and implemented in ways that undercut their original vision. Longitudinal studies indicate that, generally speaking, children benefitted from their Head Start experience but those findings are far from robust and justify the hypothesis that the way these programs were created set drastic limits to the level and strength of the benefits.

5. In the late 1960s Yale created the Institution for Social and Policy Studies (ISPS) which, like the earlier Institute of Human Relations, was a nondepartmental setting intended to bring together social scientists in an effort to contribute to an integration of practical and research knowledge relevant to the major problems of the times. I agreed to be housed there. I was the only one who had been part of IHR and knew something of its creation and fate. There were two reasons I agreed to participate, but the one most relevant here is that I had already formulated a conceptualization of the creation of settings and I did not want to pass up the opportunity to observe the creation of a setting. I can be very brief: Almost everything I described about IHR describes what happened at and to ISPS. There was an additional benefit to being part of ISPS: As a result of its internal conflicts and external critics one part of ISPS (The Center on Management) was severed from ISPS and led to the creation of Yale's School of Management. The story was the same. The School of Management was and is a battlefield on which gets played out a variety of power struggles effectively blotting out memory of the original, distinctive vision of the school.

The above accounts explain why in the early sixties I decided that I had to experience in a very personal way what is involved in creating a setting. I started and for 7 years directed the Yale Psycho-Educational Clinic. It was the most stimulating and rewarding experience of my professional life (Sarason, 1988); it gave me the basis for writing *The Creation of Settings and the Future Societies* (1972). Charter schools were not, of course, even on the horizon when I wrote the book, but when they did appear on the horizon, I knew they were a kind of acid test of my formulations. Therefore, in the next chapter I shall summarize that formulation, which is less a formulation than a set of *predictable* problems which all new settings confront but which few recognize. I italicize "predictable" advisedly because I consider those problems glimpses of the obvious; they are not arcane problems, but if not early confronted, the distinctive vision and purpose of the new setting will not be realized, proving once again that the more things change, the more they remain the same. And that assertion-prediction holds for charter schools.

CHAPTER 4

Predictable Features and Problems

The main thrust of this chapter is that the fate of a new setting is largely, but not exclusively, determined in what I label as the pre-history or the before-the-beginning stage of the new setting; that is to say, before it is operational. What happens in the first operational year is also significant because in that year the original vision and purpose collide with reality. Fantasy, vision, purpose, and planning are one thing, but the realities of implementation are another thing. Whether or not that collision is destabilizing depends on how clearly the predictable problems were recognized in the before-the-beginning phase.

Superiority and Uniqueness

No one seeks to create a new setting that will be a replica of an existing one. In some way or ways the new setting will be superior to, better than, more distinctive than comparable settings. The new setting is intended to demonstrate that its end "product" will be an improvement over comparable settings. In a purely psychological-phenomenological sense the new setting will be more than distinctive, it will be unique, it will not be a clone of comparably labeled settings. Its uniqueness may be a new idea, mode of organization, quality of end product (material or human), and the qualitative benefits members of the new setting will experience. It is the sense of uniqueness that is so powerfully motivating and captivating to the creators-leaders. It is that same sense of envisioned uniqueness that causes creators-leaders to be almost exclusively future oriented. Initially at least, they are far more clear about what the new setting will look like and accomplish than they are about what they will have to do, the resources they will need, and the time it will require to achieve their purposes. They know this in an abstract way, but they are so captivated by their vision of the future and the power of their sense of uniqueness that they hope and believe that with the "right" kind of people and resources attaining operational status will not present difficult problems. It is an exaggeration to say that the creators-leaders see the road ahead as paved with engineering issues, but it is not an exaggeration to say that they see that road as a straightforward one requiring the garnering and organizing of human and material resources.

External Constraints on Creators-Leaders

Far more often than not the new setting emerges from and is embedded in a larger existing organization which has decided a new setting is necessary or desirable. That decision may come about because someone has convinced the organization that such a new setting would enhance it and that he or she should create and direct it; or the decision is made because the person appropriate to lead it is available. Although the new setting is embedded in the larger organization, the new setting is seen as independent for all practical purposes. The point here is two-fold. First, there is verbal agreement about why the new setting is being created and what it will accomplish. Second, there is verbal agreement about what resources will be available to it. At this stage there is no thought to the maxims that "the hand that feeds you is the hand that can starve you" or "those who empower you are those who can disempower you." All is sweetness and light, there is no reason to expect serious problems. No one asks what will or might happen if there is change in leadership of the larger organization or there will have to be a decrease in support for the new setting; or as is frequent, the new setting requires more support than was expected. There is another factor rooted in organizational realities: one can never assume that the decision to create the new setting was happily greeted by all people of varying power in the larger organization. Some will see the new setting from a zero-sum stance: what the new setting gets, the older parts lose. Some will see the new setting as "privileged," as enjoying a freedom they do not have. Some will see it as an implied criticism of their part in the larger organization. The leader of the new setting may know all of this—he or she has experienced life in a complicated organization or system—but that knowledge is overwhelmed by the enthusiasm and optimism with which that person greets the opportunity to create the new setting. He or she is preoccupied with the future, with what needs to be done, with what will be, not with present or past organizational history, traditions, and what I call organizational craziness: the omnipresent struggles around power, status, and resources.

I am not asserting that any or all of the above will play an important, negative role in the creation and development of the new setting. I do assert that what I have described are *potentially* powerful external constraints on the new settings, especially because the leader of the new setting ignores them or does not devise means to keep the potential constraints from becoming actual ones. It is beyond my purposes to suggest how these potential constraints can be contained. But it is central to my purpose here to say that almost all leaders of new settings I have known have said that they belatedly learned that preoccupation with the internal development of the new setting blinded them to the importance of potential sources of constraint. As one of these leaders said to me, "I didn't realize that I should have been not only secretary of internal affairs but foreign affairs as well."

I have discussed potential sources of constraint coming from the larger organization in which the new setting is embedded. In the large and sprawling arena of the human services the external constraints on a new setting which is not embedded in a larger organization are far more actual than potential; more correctly, the potential becomes actual very quickly. For example, in the mid-sixties one of the War on Poverty programs resulted in the creation of new community agencies in urban areas the purpose of which was to develop new and better programs for poor, underserved populations. I was involved in Community Progress Incorporated (CPI) programs in New Haven. Two things were clear from the start. First, CPI would serve the inner city in ways that the traditional social agencies had not and could not serve. Indeed, the leader of CPI said to me that he wanted to stay as far away as possible from any meaningful relationship with those agencies which he regarded as dinosaurs. Second, those social agencies saw CPI as a competitor for resources and as having an antiprofessional stance. Each had disdain for the other. Each wished the other would go away. Almost from day one it was CPI versus a variety of social agencies. The fact is that CPI could have benefitted from some of the agencies' expertise, but its stance was such and it was so preoccupied with its internal development that it never sought to deal with those agencies. But it was also a fact that those agencies felt left out, criticized, rejected. CPI had a hostile surround which it could ill afford. I cannot say that if CPI had paid more sensitive attention to those agencies, to "foreign affairs," that some of its problems (which were many) would have been less severe. But I can say its stance made for constraints on what it wished to accomplish. Many of the War on Poverty programs had a short checkered career, and at their root was the lack of any conception about the minefield the creation of settings has to traverse in today's communities. Legislation, money, enthusiasm, and the most laudable goals in no way guarantee that new settings will develop and survive. I urge the reader to consult Moynihan's *Maximum Feasible Misunderstanding* (1969).

Another instructive example are the hundreds of Youth Bureaus spawned by federal and state legislation. Youth Bureaus were never intended to provide direct service to young people but rather to interconnect existing independent community social agencies each of whom had programs for young people. Blumenkrantz (1992) has well described how existing agencies resented and resisted any such role for the Youth Bureaus which they regarded as interlopers as well as reflective of an implied criticism that their programs could have greater impact by more connections among agencies. Blumenkrantz had been director of a Youth Bureau for a decade, and his personal account conveys the force of the external constraints which made achieving the mission of his new setting impossible. The Youth Bureau became still another of many agencies having its own direct service programs. Belatedly, Blumenkrantz learned that cooperative planning and pooling of ideas and resources were exercises in futility to which those who wrote the legislation had been grossly insensitive.

From the standpoint of the creation of settings the issue is not clarified by a "good guy vs. bad guy" dichotomy. The issue is that those who create new settings cannot ignore, as they almost always do, that by coming into existence the new setting will not be viewed neutrally or positively by all individuals and agencies in the community surround. Matters are not helped any if the leader of the new setting publicly proclaims that it has a more innovative, better, more important mission than existing agencies. Such proclamations may very well be true, but it carries a price: They flush out those individuals and agencies who, for one or another reason, will resent such a message and will seek ways to constrain the new setting. That price is not recognized because the leader of the new setting is so drawn to the future and the internal development of the setting that he or she pays little or no attention to "foreign affairs."

Time Perspective, Time as Enemy

I have known leaders of new settings who knew that there were external individuals and agencies who were potential critics of and constraints on the new setting but had never given thought to how the potential might be prevented from becoming actual or, at least, diluting the force of the actual when it might surface. In these instances, the single most important factor that caused the leader to pay little attention to such thinking and actions was time. That is to say, he or she comes quickly to perceive that the process of creating a new setting involves so many minor and major steps and problems that there is little or no time to deal with other than matters of internal development. That is especially the case when a date has been set (or required) for the new setting to open its doors. For most leaders this is the first time they have had the responsibility to create a new setting; they "grew up" in developed settings the characteristics of which made the creation of a new one so alluring. In the abstract they knew that time is a limited, precious resource, but it is only when they begin confronting the realities of creating a new setting, does the abstraction take on personal meaning; time does not pass, it seems to fly. The external surround recedes. Its potential for creating later problems gets little attention. The psychological here and now rivets on "getting things going," on "tooling up," and the external surround recedes more and more in to the background.

Let me paraphrase what creators of settings have said to me: "I get the import of your questions. You are implying that I and my colleagues should have dealt with a variety of individuals and agencies whom we knew might, for one or another reason, take a dim view of what we were creating and why. You are suggesting that we should have made a serious effort to get them on our side, to listen to their views, and to do this sincerely and respectfully. Today, now that we have become operational, I agree with you. We would not have some of the bedeviling problems we now have. But if we were having this discussion in the months before we opened, I would have said that you didn't understand how much time it would have taken to do what you seem to be suggesting we should have done, and that you were assuming the payoff would be worth it. Looking back, however, I would do things differently. We might, and I emphasize *might*, have made life easier for ourselves."

I quite agree with the use of the word *might*; there are no guarantees that dealing with potential sources of external criticism and constraint will be successful. But I have known of too many instances where not dealing with those sources early on aborted the creation of the setting, and there are even more instances where those sources, either in the before-the-beginning phase or in the early operational phase, influenced the new setting in ways that undercut or altered what was distinctive about the new setting. Time is a precious commodity the use of which has to rest on a dispassionate judgment of who in the external surround may come to be an obstacle to the mission of the new setting. And, as some leaders will attest, some of those external sources come later to confirm the maxim that "with friends like that we have no need of enemies."

I am sure that the reader has already concluded that I regard the creation of a setting as both a kind of once-in-a-lifetime challenge and opportunity as well as an extraordinarily trying one. To engage in the venture with the expectation that a good idea, motivation, and enthusiasm will be sufficient, that our social-institutional world will be hospitable or easily bendable to the needs of the venture, that the success of the venture will depend solely or even primarily on its internal characteristics, is illusory; such expectations contribute to disillusionment, and what is predictably trying becomes even more so. There is no way the creation of a setting can avoid being a trying one. I do believe that when we begin to appreciate (indeed acknowledge) what creating a setting entails, the rate of failure will decrease. Let us go on to other features which in their own ways are as crucial as they can be trying.

The Core Group

Choosing a core group who will play major roles in the creation of the new setting is the first task of the leader. When the new setting is but a *possibility* in the leaders's mind, that person has discussed the possibility with colleagues who the leader thinks will be supportive (at least) and perhaps would want to be part of the possible new venture. As we know, the word gets around and the number of people who approach the leader may be considerable because they view the possible new setting as more interesting and fulfilling than the one in which they are now working. Once it is made public that in fact the new setting will be created, the number of interested individuals further increases. Up until that time the leader may have tentatively decided whom he or she would want to have in the core group: those who will have major positions of responsibility. Once it is publicly known that the new setting will be created, the leader gets "down to business" with those he wants to attract. He talks individually with each of them. Although usually unnecessary, the leader unreflectively adopts a "selling" stance which almost always (I would say always) conveys several messages: The new setting will be one happy family, the person will have the opportunity to implement the unique mission of the setting, personal and intellectual rewards and recognition will be considerable. This, of course, is what the person wants to hear. It is very understandable that these discussions are suffused with goodwill and high hopes. But it is almost always the case that these initial discussions lack substantive detail. That it to say, there is little or no discussion about governance and structure and style, resources and their allocation, development of constituencies, criteria by which to judge progress, and the role the core members will play in choosing the additional staff which will be needed. The implicit assumption is that once the core group has been chosen matters of sub-stance and organization will get clarified. The other implicit assumption is that the core group and the leader are in such agreement about the sig-nificance of the goals of the setting that any disagreements that may come up will be satisfactorily resolved.

Not always, but very often the members of the core group know each other at varying levels of intimacy. If they know each other, it may be they have never worked together. And to assume that they like and respect each other is to indulge wish fulfillment. How they regard each other depends in part on how much of a voice each member had in selecting their coun-terparts. If the leader independently and serially selected the members, it becomes difficult for any of them to voice reservations about the choices; the disjunction between what one thinks and what one can say can have untoward consequences. Nor does the *order* in which the members were chosen go unnoticed. Like it or not, we all live in a world where we are made sensitive to symbols of importance and status. Choosing a core group may be a narrowly conceived personnel task, but it has or can have personal and interpersonal consequences which surface later, depending on the style and sensitivity of the leader (which I will amplify in a later section).

Once the core group has been selected, there follows a series of meetings about how to develop the setting consistent with its innovative purposes. What should be the first, second, and third steps? Where the housing of the new setting has already been decided, who will have what space for the functions for which he or she will be responsible? When housing has to be located, what locations are available and by what criteria should they be assessed? In light of available fiscal resources, what would be an acceptable compromise? When and by what procedures and criteria will such additional staff be chosen? Who will participate in selection? What can we do to avoid actions that are inconsistent with our purpose? The questions are many (if not endless) if only because creating a setting is a process in which one goes from an idea to an envisioned complicated reality in which a ruling principle is that solving one problem gives birth to new ones.

It is at these meetings when it becomes apparent that the members of the core group *and* the leader may not be in agreement about many things. Some of the core group may find that their conception of the new setting is not the same as that originally conveyed by the leader. Some may conclude that the leader is more attentive to and influenced by one or two members of the group. And it is inevitable that each core member begins to make judgments about the adequacy, judgment, trustworthiness of the other members. The extent and consequences of these judgments are largely determined by the leader's sensitivity, style, and interpersonal skills. What I am describing is complicated, subtle, tricky business, which does not mean that the consequences are always serious or lethal. But I have to say that of all the troubled settings I have known, observed, or read about, it was dynamics, composition, and conduct of those early planning meetings where the seeds of trouble were sown, and they did not sprout until some time later. Creating a setting is an intellectual and interpersonal affair, and we should not be surprised that it brings to the fore the best and the worst of people. Humans are social animals, which is to say that in their commerce with each other the manifestation of their assets and deficits will vary considerably, especially if the process and context is one they have never before confronted.

Leaders

There are parents who should not be parents, physicians who should not be physicians, teachers who should not be teachers, and psychologists (or psychiatrists) who should not be treating patients. And the same is true for leaders of organizations, especially if the organization is one yet to be created and which by design is intended to be distinctive and better than other organizations, an intention the leader has never had to actualize. Management theorists and researchers say that there are leaders who are effective only if the economy is robust and change, restructuring, and sacrifice are not necessary; there are other leaders whose style is tailor made for periods of economic recession. So, I will amend what I said above by saying that a leader of a new setting that has failed of its purposes or went out of existence *may* be more successful in leading a chronologically mature organization. The important point is that there be a match between the leader and the requirements of a new setting. Most leaders of the new setting are self-selected because the conception was theirs, they have given time and energy to gain support for the venture, and they appear to have the appropriate administrative skills. Those who "officially" appoint the essentially self-selected leader have as little experience with or knowledge of the process and problems of creating a new setting as the person they appoint.

Let us begin with a deceptively simple question. Why does the person seek to create a new setting? The person will say that he or she wants to demonstrate that his or her innovative ideas and vision will not only prove to be superior to the outcomes of more traditional settings but will cause these other settings to change. It will be a demonstration that the particular field will be unable to ignore. I make no judgment how realistic those ideas and visions are. That is not the issue here. The issue is the degree of strength of the different motivations powering the seeking of leadership. It is understandable if conceiving of the necessity and importance of a new setting gives you a sense of ownership, of understanding, of competence in regard to overseeing the effort. It is also understandable if you wish to be recognized and applauded for the success of the venture; you may consider it unseemly to express that wish to others but the wish is always there. The wish for anonymity is of zero strength in those who seek leadership. And it is also understandable if the sense of ownership motivates you to protect your ideas and role against criticism and change regardless of whether they are well intentioned or not. And precisely because it is highly likely that you have never created a setting before, you will strive to keep your doubts, insecurities, and anxieties to yourself, masking them by a display of confidence and the possession of a clear direction. And no one who seeks leadership believes that he or she lacks the skills to "handle people": To motivate them, to gain their loyalty, to get the best out of them, to forge a happy family in which everyone gives and gets. It is also a belief that one can handle situations in which members of the family in some ways interfere with "smooth" functioning of the setting.

Thousands of books have been written about leaders and leadership. Little in that literature is about leaders of new settings and what there is is retrospective in nature, the retrospection coming years after the setting was created or went out of existence. There is little about the complicated phenomenology of leaders of new settings, what in my 1972 book I have called the "socialization of the leader." From what I have read, personally experienced, and learned from the experience of others who have started new settings, there are several factors or attributes on each of which leaders vary and *in combination* vary even more from a positive to a negative extreme.

1. Power or authority is an omnipresent motive, although self-imposed controls over its manifestation can mask its strength. There are leaders in whom the power motive is so strong and unacknowledged as to justify characterizing their actions as an "ego trip." There are other leaders whose personal doubts, insecurities, or morality are so evident as to cause others to view him or her as lacking leadership qualities. I say *morality* because some of these people experience the display of power as the equivalent of an unwarranted expression of hostility, as a departure from the strictures of morality.
2. There is always a disjunction between what a leader thinks and feels about others in the setting and what the leader will say publicly. Some leaders strive to maintain a sense of treasured privacy and are almost totally unaware of how this is seen and interpreted and reacted to by others. On the other extreme some leaders make a fetish of "openness" and are puzzled by the consternation and problems it engenders in others.
3. Leaders vary considerably (I would say wildly) in how sensitive they are to criticism, how they control the display of their sensitivity, and their tendency to interpret criticism as a general attack on their competence and ideas. Some leaders are incapable of admitting a weakness or mistake. Some are so insecure that they seek to mollify a critic by too readily accepting the criticism (and often their advice).
4. Because of the strength of the "happy family" fantasy, some leaders cannot accept the reality that there will always be problems, functions, and disagreements and slowly take actions which distance themselves from what is going on in the setting. On the other extreme are leaders who

accept the reality but do not want to live with it: The leaders leave the setting. There are, albeit a few, leaders who accept the reality, deal with it forthrightly, and do not unduly blame themselves for problems that recur again and again. As one leader said, "I agree with President Truman. If it is too hot in the kitchen, get the hell out. I'm staying in this kitchen and taking the heat."

5. Creating a setting is a process which makes it very easy to forget that there is an external surround containing individuals and agencies who are potential sources of constraint. There are leaders who initially know that but soon forget it as they become more and more riveted on the myriads of problems with which the new setting confronts them. And then there are those leaders who begin to distance themselves from the setting by frequent forays into that surround as much to deal with "foreign affairs" as to avoid experiencing the surfeit of problems many of which are instances of problem creation through problem solution.

None of these factors is discrete. They become interrelated in varying ways and strengths at different times. They are called into play when the leader selects and organizes the core group; when additional staff come on board; when a long series of meetings is held where the whys, wherefores, methods, governing rules put flesh on the bones of the abstractions contained in its distinctive mission; when the pressures and stresses increase as opening day looms; when after opening day it becomes apparent that not every contingency was planned for and that some aspects of the planning had been inadequate; when the realities of being operational put limits on collegiality and rational thinking; when the functions of each part of the organization become less aware of other parts and the overall mission is no longer the sole source of purpose and mission. Throughout this developmental process the actions and behavior of everyone, including the leader, play both a cause and effect role. The socialization of the leader does not take place in a social vacuum, and that is no less true for everyone else. The actions and behavior of the leader are more pervasive and percolating than those of anyone else, but that should not obscure the fact that the actions and behavior of the leader are in part determined by what others say or do. A stimulus-response psychology to describe and understand what happens and why is utterly inadequate. If creating a setting is a horrendously—I use that word advisedly—complicated affair, so is the task of describing and comprehending what is going on and why. Indeed, the reason so many new settings fail of their purposes is that they underestimate the complexity they will encounter. Precisely because they never created a new setting, they have no conceptual road map by which to proceed. That is why leaders cling so dearly to the belief that goodwill and strong motivation will somehow or other allow them to overcome any and all obstacles.

We are used to hearing that the leader sets the "tone" of the setting. There is truth to that, but it is incomplete and even misleading. It is true in the sense that leaders do seek to set the tone, but if the leader expects that the tone will be interpreted and reacted to in the same way by everyone else, it can cause problems, minor or major. To confuse intent with accomplishment is a folly to which many leaders are victims. If eternal vigilance is the price we pay for liberty, eternal sensitivity is the price the leader pays to avoid the consequences of failing to take seriously that the tone he or she hears and projects is not the one *everyone* else has. That is a price that leaders on an ego trip are not able or willing to pay; deviations from the tone are regarded as inherently threatening, not a basis for self-questioning but rather a basis of criticism directed to others.

When we say the leader sets the tone, we ordinarily intend to convey in a shorthand way an overall affective feature of a setting: friendly, sullen, relaxed, tense, buoyant, subdued, etc. It is a way of characterizing the quality of relationships in the setting. However, precisely because a new setting is justified in terms of new ideas and concepts—it will be an improvement over comparable settings—tone is never independent of how clearly those ideas are articulated, examined, reexamined. Regardless of whether the setting is new or old, it will be comprised of people whose personalities—temperament—are not, to indulge understatement, made for each other. In a new setting there is the additional burden of two factors. The first is that few, if anyone, in the setting (including the leader) have ever been part of creating a new setting. Second, the new ideas and concepts are just that: new, not yet implemented in a surround over which the creators have relatively little control, an unpredictable world. Those two factors are sources of anxiety and pressure. How those sources are recognized and dealt with interact with other sources of interpersonal differences.

I trust the reader will now understand why I said that creating a setting is not for everyone who grasps the opportunity to do so. I will have more to say about this at the end of this chapter. At this point I turn to a feature that is bedeviling and whose impact and importance are either underestimated or miscalculated or both. Here, too, the lack of previous experience in creating distinctive new settings plays its usual, disruptive role.

Resources

I begin with my late cousin whose job was to estimate the cost of large buildings or housing developments. And by cost was meant the value of everything that would be needed to meet design-architectural specifications, ranging from labor to types of door knobs, to stair railings. He had to estimate costs for literally hundreds of items. The reason, of course, was so that the builder-developer would know the total cost in order to set a selling (or rental) price that would permit him to make a profit. Large developers have learned the hard way that off-the-cuff estimates of costs can lead to unacceptable loss and bankruptcy. And they also have learned that the accuracy of estimates is imperilled if determined by those emotionally involved in the venture. Accuracy requires not only knowledge but a kind of obsessive attention to detail. My cousin was a well-paid estimator with an excellent track record. Builders-developers trusted his estimates. He would be given the task, he would carry it out (it could take months), and he would be unconcerned about whether the builder-developer "liked" the estimates. Frequently, they did not like the estimates, and they would sit with him to determine where changes in design and specifications might lower the overall cost. I truly began to appreciate the demands of his assignments when, around the time New York's World Trade Center opened, a long article appeared in the *New York Times* on what had been involved and how long it took to estimate the cost of those skyscrapers; no one person did it or could have done it.

Creating a new setting requires estimation (not educated guesses) about the resources that will be needed. Let us assume that putting up a building will not be necessary or is simply out of the question because of limited resources. Even so, how to use or redivide or renovate existing space takes time and money, and if changes in plumbing, lighting, and electrical wiring will be needed the costs are not paltry. Depending on the nature and purposes of the new setting the number of physical changes that you feel desirable or necessary can be considerable so that what you judged to be an adequate budget proves to be otherwise. These and other miscalculations about the physical space become significant to the extent that they impact on funds budgeted for human resources: number of staff, salaries, and benefits; computer and duplicating services; books and subscriptions to professional-technical journals; travel to meetings; and more. In the minds of the creators the imagery of the new setting may not have deserved the label luxurious, but neither did it suggest one that would be uncongenial to the *purposes* of the different people in the setting. I italicize *purposes* because people may be willing to adjust to the physical aspects of the space if it is aesthetically unattractive but when it interferes with the purposes of one's functions, it is another story, especially if it appears that these interferences will not disappear in the future.

Whether any of the above factors or possibilities will become sources of personal or interpersonal grievance depends on what I call governance:

By whom and in what types of forums are decisions made? Resources, human or fiscal, are limited and must be allocated by criteria that at best only minimally jeopardize the setting's purposes. The style and formal ways by which resources are allocated are from very early on a source of the greatest interest to everyone in the setting; no one is neutral about those ways, everyone judges those ways in terms of the importance they attach to their individual responsibilities. If they have no role in decision making and/or they regard the decisions as wrong and misguided or, worse yet, a reneging on promises made, the seeds of discontent are planted and how quickly they grow (if they do) depends on the dynamics or factors I have discussed in previous sections. That is why I said what I did about the utter inadequacy of a stimulus-response explanation of what happens in a new setting. It is as if everything is related, both as cause and effect, to everything else, and to attribute cause x to effect y may satisfy the need for simple explanations but at the expense of sensitivity to or recognition of a complicated web of relationships in which any one factor does not, cannot, have encapsulated consequences. Those consequences may be observable or not, and their significance may not be understood until their connections to other goings on are triggered by a seemingly unrelated event, decision, or conflict.

Creating a new setting is a complicated affair which can become quite messy long before the setting becomes operational. Messiness is not an inherently negative feature except when those who are creating the setting bring with them the fantasy that love and strong motivation, plus laudably distinctive purposes, and a belief in a benevolent goddess of luck will be sufficient to overcome whatever problems they will encounter. And if in addition they have a most rosy picture of a happy family comprised of people not possessed of ambivalence, personal agendas, undue frailties, or a low level of frustration tolerance, the betting odds for failure are high. If anything is predictable in creating a new setting, it is that there will be unpredictable problems ahead, not only because it is new but that it is new with new distinctive purposes never before experienced by its creators and those they bring on board. As my late cousin said to me, "When I get a job to estimate a new building which has many innovative features an architect has conned the developer to incorporate in the specifications, I can go nuts. As soon as I start estimating what these innovations will require, really what they may require, I am tempted to say to the developer no thank you. What I do when I am through is to warn him that there is a margin of error probably larger than I think and that he had better think twice about how to figure his final, overall costs."

Most readers will have had no experience with charter schools and will regard them as a kind of new species to which their knowledge and experience have no relevance. That is understandable but such readers are selling themselves short. That is unfortunate because most readers, if only because they read newspapers and magazines, know about mergers in the private and nonprofit sectors in society. By definition a merger is an example of the creation of a new setting in order to achieve agreed-upon goals which each alone could not do. It is a form of marriage; the smallest instance of a new setting. A merger, like marriage, requires far more than the pooling of resources if the agreed-upon goals are to be achieved. Therefore, in the next chapter I shall discuss two mergers in the hope that it will serve as a helpful prologue to the subsequent chapters on charter schools. Mergers and charter schools are on the surface in different worlds but they share very similar developmental dynamics. Up until recent decades schools were regarded as unique institutions. It is one thing to say they are unique and, therefore, incomparable. It is another thing to say they are different, that they share important features with other complicated organizations. Similarly, mergers and charter schools are, from the standpoint of the creation of settings, not in different worlds. I trust, therefore, that the reader will not view the next chapter as irrelevant to the focus of this book.

CHAPTER 5

Mergers as Creations of Settings

Mergers, as the reader well knows, have been taking place at a somewhat exponential rate in almost all spheres of social-institutional activity, e.g., business, health, publishing, to name but a few. However explicit and varied the stated purposes of the merger may be, there is one purpose that is bedrock: The merged organization will be "better" than and "superior" to what the two organizations had heretofore been.

That was the case in the merger of two hospitals very near each other, literally across the street from each other. The merging of the two hospitals would make them more competitive with other health organizations, to survive, and to exploit their existing resources more efficiently. There was another feature characteristic of the creation of a new setting. The merger was spearheaded by the leaders of the two hospitals. In my 1972 book I talk of the new setting only in terms of a single leader. What I did not but should have stressed is that in all of the illustrative cases I referred to—including my leadership in creating the Yale Psycho-Educational Clinic—the leader is always dealing with other leaders, so that in my case I had to deal with the chairman, the dean of the graduate school, and the provost at Yale. In a more indirect way I also had to deal with leaders of community agencies. It was a mistake on my part to convey the impression that the leader of a new setting operates without constraint on some Olympian perch. In the book I emphasize that he or she is constrained by the human dynamics within the setting. I did not (and could not) envision that a time would soon come when leaders of two settings would agree so frequently to participate in the creation of a new setting.

There is a difference between mergers and absorptions as in the case of hostile takeovers where there is no intention of creating a new setting. Mergers are instances of creating a new setting which are expected to benefit both parties as in the case of the smallest instance of the creation of a new setting: marriage. I know that asserting entering marriage involves issues and dynamics similar to those in a willing corporate merger may strike some people as strange, as equating apples and oranges, but close scrutiny of the marriage-divorce literature (a voluminous one) and the burgeoning one on mergers reveals compelling similarities in substance and process. The expectation of better or superior consequences; the belief that motivation and goodwill are sufficient to overcome obstacles; that verbal agreement on values and purposes means the same thing to the participants; that little or no significant issues surrounding leadership and power will emerge; that personal differences in style, ambition, and future perspective among the participants will be secondary to the overarching concern for the welfare of the setting; that people or forces external to the setting but who are interested in or impacted directly or indirectly by the new setting will not be threats to it; that there are or will be sufficient resources to surmount all difficulties; that whatever problems or conflicts occurred in the "before-the-beginning" phase have been resolved and will not reappear—these are some of the more obvious commonalities between mergers and marriages. You can sum up much of this in this way: The enthusiasm, the fantasy of enduring good will and accomplishment of "success," blot out attention to (or mammothly downplay) *predictable* problems to any venture in which people come together over a sustained period of time to achieve agreed-upon goals. That, it is obvious, is true for marriage, and I predict, it will be no less characteristic of mergers.

Back to the merger of the two hospitals. For a period of years I was a member of an external advisory committee to one of those hospitals which had a deserved national reputation for the quality of its research, patient care, and the level of job satisfaction of *all* its employees. Indeed, in a list of the 30 "corporations" reputed to have the highest level of employee satisfaction, this was the only hospital on the list. This did not surprise me because over the years I had met with laundry staff, kitchen help, nurses, ward attendants, lab technicians, physicians, and more. Although the hospital opposed union efforts to organize it, it never went to anything resembling an extreme effort to block or undermine the union's activities. The union has never won an election. I am not alone in the belief that the president-leader of the hospital is in a class by himself in regard to interpersonal sensitivity, direct contact with and direct knowledge of employee feelings, attitudes, and advice (and this is a large hospital in a large city renowned for its hospitals).

When I received the agenda for the most recent meeting, it contained the announcement that we will discuss an agreed-upon merger with a very nearby hospital. Being a devoted reader of the *New York Times* and diverse periodicals, I was aware (how could one not be?) of what has been called "merger mania" and had regretted the fact that I had no opportunity to observe any aspect of the merger process. Some of the accounts I had read were of the gory variety in regard to the turmoil and animosities that preceded and followed the mergers. Needless to say, where a merger has been relatively successful, depending on what you consider to be criteria of success, you are not likely to hear about it if only because it is not considered newsworthy. We know far more about failed than about successful marriages, and that is likely to turn out to be the case in regard to mergers.

In any event, I eagerly looked forward to the meeting. I wrote down several questions to which I hoped I might get at least a partial answer.

1. Who would assume leadership of the merged settings? What was the basis for that choice? Was the decision arrived at without difficulty? Were its implications, near and long term, examined in an explicit and forthright manner? How explicit were the altered powers of the new and supplanted leadership? In the event that problems of power and leadership arise, what mechanisms or forums would exist to deal with them? Or was it that there was no recognition of the possibility that such problems were predictable, or if they did arise, was the feeling that they could be overcome by good will, reason, and selflessness? Was it the case that issues of leadership reflected the strength and role of the two boards of trustees and, to a lesser extent, the two present leaders? In brief, who participated and in what ways in the decision?

2. Immediately below the two top leaders and their boards, each hospital had a far from minuscule layer of leaders-managers. What role and when did these people participate in the decision to merge? Among these layers in each hospital, what degree of agreement was obtained about the merger? What questions, problems, predictions, concerns surfaced, and what alternatives, not to the merger itself, but to the details of the agreement were expressed? Were they presented as a *fait accompli*, and if so, were there "symptoms" of resentment, fear, puzzlement about an altered future that may or may not include them?

3. In any hospital its health professionals, especially physicians and nurses, are, to say the least, protective of their status, recognition, and prerogatives. (And these were two teaching, university-affiliated hospitals!) One does not have to be a semi-sage to say that these professionals would not view the merger with other than deep concern. I do not feel it is necessary to list the questions the merger aroused in their minds.

4. From my perspective the group that would feel the most concern would also be the largest: the diverse non- or semi-professionals who are the least powerful, the most expendable, the least educated or skilled. Here, again, it is not necessary to list what went through their minds when they learned of the merger.

The two institutions were hospitals, but they had two different cultures and traditions. That they were similar in many ways goes without saying, but just as two elementary schools, or two universities, or two families have some common characteristics, they each have a distinctive feel, "soul," ambience, and self-definition. As I said earlier, the hospital on whose advisory committee I served regarded itself and was so regarded by others (locally and nationally) as distinctive bordering on unique. This, I should hasten to add, is no put down of the other hospital but rather as a way of saying that they were "psychologically" two different settings. In my book I emphasized that the leader gathers around him or her a "core group" which, however devoted to the stated purposes of the new setting, is comprised of different *individuals, personalities with personal-professional experience.* These differences inevitably loom larger in practical import after the creation of the setting than before. That is old hat to people who marry and who may have known each other, or even have lived with each other, for a considerable time before marriage. Merging two cultures is, of course, exponentially more complicated. I felt safe in assuming that each hospital knew itself in a way it did and could not know the other.

What were the stated purposes of the merger? Those purposes were not easy to come by, in part because the immediate purpose was so obvious: In a quickly changing health care scene in which economic competition from insurance companies and HMOs was approaching cut throat intensity, the merging of two highly regarded hospitals made the survival of each far more likely at the level and with the quality consistent with past performance. I knew that in the preceding year "my" hospital had conducted the possibility of a merger with at least one other major hospital but that discussion proved fruitless for reasons never made clear to me. It was not a good "match"; the problems were too many and thorny. The merger with the nearby hospital apparently was less fraught with predictable difficulties because the major strengths of each were somewhat different, each could add to the strengths of the other, each would become better and stronger. There was another purpose and that was that each hospital would be minimally impacted, its "character" would not change except minimally, i.e., in relatively unimportant ways (unspecified).

It would be unfair to say that the leader of the hospital conveyed the impression to us that the merger would not be beset by thorny problems. But it is not unfair to say that he truly felt that those problems would not be disruptive, that there was a degree of goodwill and clarity of understanding that would overcome what difficulties would be encountered. He expressed no reservations. Given what I have written about what a frail reed good will, good intentions, and enthusiasm-optimism are as insurance in the creation of a setting, my skepticism was not assuaged. *It is insurance, but it is of the short term variety.*

It was during the discussion that the obvious dawned on me: The public announcement of the merger had already introduced a new dynamic in the cultures of the two hospitals. Indeed, rumors of the proposed merger had surfaced before the final decision had been made. What the formal announcement did was galvanize everyone to confront and think about a new future which conceivably would alter plans, hopes, ambitions, working conditions—let alone the possibility that you will not be in that institutional future. I do not say that on the basis of any interviewing I or anyone else did but rather as a glimpse of the obvious for which no interviewing is necessary. What I say is one thing, what those who are managing the merger *need* to know in a very concrete way is quite another thing. There was no indication that any special efforts were being made to sample and respond to the concerns and questions, to give people the feeling that those concerns and questions were important, expected, and would be dealt with. In this instance I must emphasize that the rumors and then the announcement had introduced a new dynamic in both hospitals the consequences of which may be minimal, moderate, or large. The point is that you must not ignore that or a similar dynamic.

The merger was one item on the agenda, and the discussion of it provided no answers to almost all of my questions. What it did provide was confirmation of two features of the process of the creation of settings derived from personal experience and observation of the creation of other settings. The first is that the creators have no guiding, systematic, conception or framework that acts as a control over the major variables in thinking and action which can contribute to failure or cause the setting to take a direction at variance with its stated purposes, i.e., the setting survives but it is not the setting that was envisioned. For example, builders of bridges have a detailed conception of how to build the structure so that it will achieve its intended purposes and will not endanger the lives of people who construct or use it. Indeed, the builders know how to calculate the predictable stresses to which the bridge will be subjected: The number of cars it can hold, the range of weather conditions at the site, the durability of materials. Having made those calculations they add a safety factor to deal with stresses discernibly beyond "normal" or predictable conditions, i.e., they know from the history of bridge building that you have to plan for usual *and* unusual conditions. Similarly, no surgeon in the two hospitals operates on the assumption that he or she will not have to alter the procedures they will employ. They have learned—it is central to their cognitive map of the human body—that what was usual in past similar cases may or may not be usual with the next patient. In fact, the operation has associated with it a number of safety factors "just in case." Safety factors are essentially preventive in the nature.

The creators of settings—certainly in the case of the hospital merger—do not have an articulate guide, map, or conception of what they have undertaken. It is not that they are flying blind, so to speak. That would be an unwarranted assertion. It is rather that they are unaware that they have not identified (a) the major aspects of the process that result in errors of omission and commission, (b) the kinds of actions that might or can reduce those errors, and (c) the resources of time and personnel which those actions require. It is (c) which in the case of the hospital merger confirmed what I said about time perspective in the creation of settings, i.e., a very unrealistic time perspective that derives from an egregious underestimation of the complexity and demands of the process. No one seeks to create a setting in a way that will defeat its purposes. But if your conception of the process is incomplete or superficial, you may achieve wisdom long after you can rectify your errors of omission or commission. "If only I had known this, or done that, or I had allowed myself more time"—these are the frequent, private reflections of almost all leaders of new settings I have known. One such person put it this way: "My enthusiasm for what we wanted to do was so strong and compelling that I was totally insensitive to the fact that I was operating according to a self-constructed time schedule that I know now was nonsensical and blotted out any sensitivity I had to warning signs that all was not going smoothly." But no less important than internal pressures to press ahead are external pressures, ranging from the requirements of funding sources which require you to present a calendar-driven schedule to which you are expected to adhere, to pressures reflective of the fact that the new setting can be expected to be subject to pressures either from diverse sources in the larger institution in which it will be embedded or from the many organizations in the geographical area who do not perceive the new setting in neutral terms, i.e., they may see themselves, directly or indirectly, now or later, as being affected by the new settings. The leaders of new settings so tend to rivet in thought and action on that setting that they pay little attention to other external settings. It is as if they divided the world into "in here" and "out there," and it is the former on which their attention rivets. That is why I paid special attention to the "before the beginning phase." It is in that phase that the role of external forces and vested interests make their appearance, unobtrusively and even non-intrusively, although once the new setting becomes a reality some of those forces and interests may become pressure and problem producing.

I said earlier that the merger was not intended to alter in any significant way the culture and character of either hospital. There would be economic-procedural changes to increase efficiency and the ability to compete, but those changes would not, we were told, dilute the health care, research, and educational performance of either. In fact, it was envisioned that the merger would very likely increase the leadership of both in the medical community; they would be better than and superior to other hospitals and to their own parts.

I regarded the belief that you can introduce economic changes and limit or isolate their impact so that the character of the setting hardly changes to be very problematic—not impossible, but highly unlikely, if only because the immediate stimulus for the merger was an economic one. More correctly, precisely because the economic factor was so obvious and strong, it is not an indulgence of pessimism to say that economic pressures have a dynamic hard to contain. And, experience indicates, when those pressures do not readily have their intended financial consequences, the scope and impact of those pressures tend to enlarge. I believe the president of the hospital knew that. But I also believe that his enthusiasm for the merger caused him to misevaluate that possibility. What if the economic changes do not achieve their intended purpose? I tried to pose that question, but given the constraints of time and the agenda the question never got answered. What was behind that question was another one: If the desired economic benefits were not forthcoming, was there agreement that additional specified economic measures would have to be taken which, however unpalatable, would have demonstrable, percolating non-economic consequences? If there was no discussion and agreement on that possibility, there was trouble ahead.

From what I have said the reader would be quite justified in feeling that I have described a problem and process that are bewilderingly complex and beset with pot holes which convince you that if given the opportunity to create a new setting, you would pass up the opportunity. Bear in mind that in this chapter I have been discussing the merger of two large, complex organizations which compared to two people entering marriage is a difference that does make a difference. But we have to ask why so many marriages fail? Granted that mergers and marriages are vastly different in scale, but that does not mean that what makes for success or failure in marriage is in theory and practice irrelevant to success or failure of mergers. I believe that the variables are identical, however different they are in scale and context.

In discussing the merger it was not my intention to suggest that it will not achieve its purposes. The fact is that I have no basis for prediction, and it is unlikely we will ever have a basis for comprehending what is happening now and its relation to what happens subsequently. I have "hunches," of course, but what is needed is the kind of longitudinal description by which to judge hunches, by which to improve or change in some important way a conception of the creation of settings. It is a conceptual problem of significant import for the practical world.

As I was writing this chapter, I found myself in the company of a woman whom I had never met before. She was a very bright, articulate, forthright, likeable person. I asked her where she worked. Her answer was that she was a senior executive for a Fortune 500 company which 2 years before had merged with another equally large company, a merger which received much play in the mass media. Interested (obsessed?) as I was in the creation of settings, I plied her with questions the thrust of which can be gleaned from the following.

1. The stimulus for the merger was economic survival but no less important was that the two companies, far from being competitors, had complementary interests and skills which would allow each to exploit those interests and skills in ways each could not do by itself. By merging they could exploit their human and material resources far better than before.
2. The heads of the two companies agreed, almost from the very start of negotiations, that (a) secrecy was crucial, (b) there should be no protracted negotiations, and (c) which of the two CEOs would head the new company. "These two people were as compatible, reasonable, and as far-seeing executives as I have ever known."
3. The reason they insisted on secrecy and speed was to prevent the level of high morale among employees from dissipating. "And by employees they meant *all* employees at *all* levels. They knew what the rumor mill could do to morale, and they did not want to feed that mill."
4. The merger and its details were agreed-upon in an amazingly short time (27 days), and the announcement was communicated to the thousands of employees, with the assurance that they would have the opportunity personally to have any of their questions discussed and answered candidly.
5. Immediately after the merger was consummated the two CEOs met with about 30,000 employees face-to-face in 62 meetings at individual plants and answered hundreds of questions many of which were brutally frank. The answers were not sugar coated.

The executive with whom I talked was Susan Pearce, Vice-President for Communication for Lockheed Martin, the two companies which merged. The only secure conclusion I could come to from our conversation was that she had no doubt that the smoothness and speed of the merger were primarily due to two people (especially the present CEO) who knew what they wanted to do and what they wanted to avoid. She pointed out that very soon after the merger the company experienced a steady, even dramatic, growth and profitability which continue to this day. Subsequent to our brief conversation (in which, I think, I came across as a prosecutor) she sent me a reprint of an article by the present CEO, Norman Augustine, with the title "Reshaping an Industry: Lockheed Martin's Survival Story" (1997). Let me comment briefly on its relevance for the creation of settings. It is a most interesting article.

Mr. Augustine presents ten rules he employed in arranging and sustaining the merger.

> Regrettably, these rules are not based on elegant, esoteric theories; they are distilled from actual experiences. Adapting to a rapidly changing business environment is not fun, and managers most assuredly should not treat it like a spectator sport. There is a saying in the world of corporate finance that every time management tries something that works, economists invariably ask, "Would it have worked in theory?" In this case, I don't know if the rules work in theory—but they worked in practice. (p. 85)

I do not know why he says "regrettably." The answer, I suspect, is implied in his phrase "elegant, esoteric theories," a kind of putdown of the role of theory for action and practice. A theory is a general, integrated set of ideas or variables intended to indicate or explain why certain occurrences "out there in the real world" have the characteristics they do, so that anyone who has to deal with those occurrences will not make the mistake of oversimplifying what he or she is dealing with. A theory, elegant or not, does not tell you what to *do* but how to *think*. That is what I tried to do in my book, to identify and to interrelate factors I considered crucial to the creation of a setting. I studiously avoided writing a manual for action. For example, it is obvious in the book that I regard the phenomenology of the leader of bedrock importance. And by phenomenology I refer to motivation, self-confidence and regard, ambition, interpersonal style, approach to planning, values, frustration tolerance. In brief, those attributes enter into what the leader does, why he does it, and how. The title of Mr. Augustine's article contains the word *story*. But his ten rules do not constitute a story, let alone one in which we get a feel for what Mr. Augustine is as a person who played a major role in the story. We get glimpses of his personality and style. For example, he has a sense of humor and the comic. He has more than his share of self-confidence but at the same time a humility comes through; he is decisive, not arrogant. He is not one whose regard for those in lower strata of the organization prevents him from "listening."

> In the 1980s, NASA challenged Lockheed Martin to cut the weight of the huge fuel tank that forms the structural backbone of the space shuttle by several thousand pounds. The effort stalled at the last 800 pounds. As the blue-ribbon

engineering team turned its attention to increasingly exotic lightweight materials—which often seemed to be derivatives of "unobtainium"—one of the line workers made a suggestion: stop painting the tank. The 200 gallons of white paint that covered the tank added 800 pounds to a device whose life span in flight was only about eight minutes and whose fate was to end up at the bottom of the Indian Ocean. Sometimes the best way to think outside the box is to listen to someone who *is* outside the box.

Even inside a company, almost every individual is a customer—a customer of coworkers. About 15 years ago at one of our electronics facilities in Orlando, Florida, the complacency bred of past success started to infect one of our manufacturing processes. Occasionally, parts were omitted from component kits prepared for assembly and inspection at another factory. Each missing part disrupted the assembly process and frustrated the workers assembling the products. I borrowed an idea from an automobile dealer in Dallas I had heard about. The dealer received few complaints from customers because he gave them the home telephone numbers of the mechanics who worked on their cars. I arranged for workers to include their names, work phone numbers, and self-addressed postcards in the kits they prepared. Complaints dropped precipitously. (p. 89)

There are more examples suggesting that Mr. Augustine is an unusual leader and human being, without whom the "story" would have been different. However, such a conclusion—more an inference than a conclusion—begs the question: What kind of a person do you have to be in order to act even semiconsistently with his ten rules? Mr. Augustine does not attempt to deal with that question, although his article contains "teasers" which whet our appetite to learn more about him. I assume he would agree that acting on his rules cannot be separated from the actor, i.e., you can agree with his rules but implementing them in the crucible of action depends on the kind of person the implementer is. I have no doubt that he could come up with a long list of colleagues he has known or observed who have agreed with the soundness of his rules but about whom Mr. Augustine would say that they know the letter of the rules but not the spirit. For example, at one point he says, "all CEOs should have in a desk drawer a list of the worst things that could happen and a set of contingency plans." I was startled by that sentence because, as I emphasize in my book, most creators of new settings tend to have a rosy picture of the future which blots out thoughts of "worst things." There are hints in the article that dealing with thoughts about "worst things" is not an encapsulated but rather a general characteristic of the way he understands and experiences his world—it is part of his "nature."

The point I am making here is one that in principle has bedeviled the arena of psychotherapy. It is an arena of "schools of psychotherapy," each of which has a distinctive theory and a set of rules about how to help troubled people. All of these schools claim effectiveness even though their theories and rules of practice are markedly different. It took years of controversy and research before it was begrudgingly recognized that perhaps the most important factor in psychotherapeutic success—independent of theory and rules—was the personality of the therapist, i.e., his or her ability to convey interest, respect, trust.

Not everyone can or should be a psychotherapist. Not everyone can or should be a doctor, lawyer, or teacher. Not everyone can or should be the creator of a new setting. I am sure Mr. Augustine knows that, although he does not talk about it. I can understand why he did not because if he had, it would appear too self-serving, or too personally revealing, or both. I say that on the basis of personal experience. I wrote the book after the Yale Psycho-Educational Clinic had been created and I had directed it for 8 years. In the book I discuss the clinic but in a *personally* unrevealing way, although in the chapter "Socialization of the Leader," I was indirectly talking about me. I knew I was not as forthcoming as I should have been and wanted to be. I made very partial amends in the chapter on the clinic in my 1988 autobiography, *The Making of an American Psychologist.*

There are some interesting differences and similarities between the two mergers I have discussed in this chapter. Both were "friendly" mergers between near equals. Both mergers were stimulated by the need to survive, but there was more to it than that because in the two mergers there was the belief that they would do more and better. In the case of Lockheed Martin their merged resources could be better exploited; in the case of the two hospitals their teaching and research activities would not only be safeguarded but deepened in scope. In both instances the leaders were charismatic and unusual people.

The differences were several. In the case of Lockheed Martin the decisions about leadership were made quickly, secretly, and with clarity. In the case of the hospitals it was clear who the leader would be, but it was also clear that there would be constraints on him, constraints the consequences of which no one seemed (at least to me) to be directly confronting. Lockheed Martin's leadership made what I consider unusual (if not heroic) and speedy efforts to communicate, through writing and personal appearances, the nature of the merger to all of its employees. That sense of urgency was missing in the hospital merger. The leader of Lockheed Martin did not underestimate the difficulty of the process; he tried to anticipate and deal with anticipated problems. In the case of the hospital merger I had to conclude that they were underestimating what lay ahead and were unprepared to deal with the predictable problems.

Nothing I have said about the two mergers is based on hard evidence. I was in no way privy to what went on in negotiations leading up to the mergers, and I was and am unable to know in *any* detail what happened afterwards. I was emboldened to discuss these mergers for three reasons: First, I wanted to stress a point I did not discuss in my 1972 book: Mergers are instances of creating a setting in that they involve two or more people in new and sustained relationships to achieve agreed-upon goals. Whether it is marriage, a national revolution, a clinic, a new Head Start site, a merger, charter schools—despite their real, apparent differences and goals they are engaged in the creation of a setting. Second, the frequency of mergers, which probably will increase in the future, will shape to an undetermined extent the nature of our society. Generally speaking, the social sciences are not all that interested in the business sector which they see and judge in narrow, economic terms. They have no theory which would allow them to see that mergers are close kin to social institutions they do study. Third, if I am correct about the social and conceptual significances of mergers, I am in no way optimistic that those significances will be studied in ways that will allow us to learn what we need to learn in order to contribute to better outcomes.

An artist friend of mine expressed some dismay about my use of the word *creation*. For him creativity is an individual characteristic, i.e., the creative individual conceives of and creates a visible or palpable "work" for the stimulation and enrichment of viewers. I asked him if all artists are creative. He said no, that artists differ markedly in creativity, ranging from a smidgeon above pedestrian to an Olympian level of creativity. How do you explain that range? I asked. That, he replied, is a mystery. I told him that the range he talked about was no different than the range I had observed among people who created settings. All creators of settings have a "picture" of what they want their peopled setting to be, how they want others to regard the setting, to value and psychologically "own it." But just as in the case of the artist (visual, literary, musical, choreographic, etc.) that the final product may be judged as a failure, partial or total, it is no different in the case of the creators of settings. But, I continued, the sources of the range among them is no *complete* mystery and that is why I wrote the book. I tried to explain a few aspects of the mystery of why some creators of settings have a personal, cognitive, and imaginative artistry that does not blind them to what they will have to do to traverse a road containing a myriad of potholes that can negatively affect the picture they had in mind.

That mystery remains I would like to be the first to acknowledge. But for me the mystery has a magnetic attraction that does not allow me to believe that the range of outcomes I have observed will always remain largely a mystery. That belief is the easy way out.

CHAPTER 6

Charter Schools

When I wrote the book in 1972, my major purpose was to indicate that creating a new setting was a frequent affair once one went beyond the different labels customarily given to such attempts. If labels are inevitable and necessary, they unwittingly reinforce the tendency to be far more attentive to differences than to commonalities among settings having different labels. Although I had deep interests in and extensive ongoing relationships with public schools, I did not discuss them in any depth in the book, and for three reasons. First, my involvement in schools focussed on how to change, improve, or reform schooling, not how to create new types of schools (Sarason, 1990, 1996). Second, the fantastic frequency with which new schools had been created in response to the baby boom caused by World War II had markedly decreased. There were, for my purposes, no descriptive accounts suitable to my needs. Third, as I shall discuss later, my rivetting on the creation of a new setting, obscured for me the fact that, more often than not, trying to change a setting required the creation of a group (i.e., leader, core group) the history dynamics and fate of which were in principle highly similar to efforts to create a new institutional setting. Not identical, but similar.

The 1972 book appeared at a time when the momentum for school reform was beginning to lose steam, to be slowly but steadily replaced by a puzzled disillusionment with the fruits of reform. As the years passed, an increasing number of people concluded that improving the quality and outcomes of schools may be a hopeless quest. Yet improvement efforts continued. Reports were published, some appearing in the mass media about a school here and a school there where schooling had been discernibly improved. But there was no evidence whatsoever that those isolated instances spread elsewhere in the system. Public, political, and professional discontent, far from abating, increased. Less than a decade ago, the concept of a charter school began to have currency. A charter school would be one created by some combination of educators, parents, and others in the community, a school for which the founding group would have *full* responsibility for its governance, organization and purposes. For each pupil the school would receive the per-pupil expenditure for a pupil in a regular public school, the amount varying for an elementary, middle, or high school student (per-pupil expenditure for a middle or high school student is higher than for one in an elementary school). Depending on the enabling legislation of the different states, continuation of a charter school would be decided after 3–5 years. The criteria for the continuation decision are stated in very general terms, although in most states the state department of education will play a key role. It is worthy of emphasis that a charter school is on its own, an independence it sought in order to improve the education of its students according to its lights, to avoid the pressures for uniformity.

The charter school movement is the most radical challenge ever to the existing system. Although it has never been stated, let alone recognized, by national and state political leadership, you do not have to be a logician to conclude that charter schools are based on the opinion that the present system is unrescuable (Sarason, 1998). That is to say, the present system is by itself incapable of reforming itself, of innovating in ways that support or do not defeat the spirit of an innovation. What the legislation says to would-be innovators is, "If you have a way of improving the quality and outcomes of schooling and you cannot implement that way within the system, here is an opportunity to get out of the clutches of the system." A majority of the state legislatures has permitted a small number of charter schools to come into existence. In the 1996 presidential campaign the president said he would ask Congress to support the creation of 3,000 more charter schools.

Charter schools are as clear examples of the creation of new settings as one will find. At the present time most charter schools are in their early phase of existence. It is fair to say that we know little of how they are doing and why, with one exception I will discuss later. In regard to the "before the beginning phase" nothing is known, as if all that preceded rolling out the welcome mat for entering students in no way did or would play a role in the life and outcomes of the school. The fact is that no legislation, national or state, included funds to observe and record in an independent, dispassionate way the "story" of the school, including the before-the-beginning phase. That did not surprise me, and for two reasons. The first is that the creation of a new school—or any new setting—is associated with imagery of organizational-engineering-administrative issues, not with conceptual, interpersonal, philosophical, interinstitutional issues. And, I repeat, it is imagery that assumes that all that went before the setting became operational is best deposited in a museum of dead history, until, of course, later developments may stimulate you to visit that museum. The second reason is that political leaders, again national or state, almost never (I would say never) support an educational initiative with the funds and means on the basis of which it can be determined how experience with model A of the initiative should be used to develop model B. They proclaim the virtues of model A as if it will not require changes, as if in the real world of human affairs a new, complicated social-educational institution will not require revision and improvement.

In 1993 K. S. Louis and J. A. King described and analyzed the creation of two new, innovative middle schools which were conceived before charter schools appeared on the scene. In all respects the creation of these two schools confirm what I have said about charter schools. The conceptual influence of Louis, as well as her article with King, is reflected in *Minnesota Charter Schools Evaluation: An Interim Report*, done in 1996 under the auspices of the Center for Applied Research and Educational Improvement at the University of Minnesota. Louis contributed to the statement of conclusions, and I take no exception to the substance of that statement. I would like to believe that the policy makers who sponsored the evaluation will take the report seriously, but candor requires that I say I will be most surprised if they act in accord with the evaluation.

I have talked at length with four individuals who are in the process of creating a charter school, i.e., they are in the before-the-beginning phase, their proposal has been approved. Without exception they described a litany of obstacles "erected" by the school system from which the charter school personnel and parents came, or from the state department of education, or from local officials, or all of these. As one of them put it, "It is as if we were creating a leper colony." Precisely because a charter school is an implicit criticism of and challenge to the existing school system, opposition to it is not surprising. In each instance the opposition took subtle, or bureaucratic, even direct form, and in each instance the direct and indirect opposition came as a surprise to the creators. Indeed, in two instances the leaders were sorry they had engaged in the venture. One of these leaders—a person who had national visibility—made it her business to seek out others who were creating charter schools. She said, "Many of these people are afraid publicly to vent their spleen about the hurdles put in their way. They are afraid of offending because it may have adverse consequences down the road." My sample of interviewees may be atypical but that is the point: Charter schools are not being created in a way that will permit us to determine how experience in the before-the-beginning phase affected the planning, morale, and cohesiveness of those responsible for these schools. I assume that charter schools will vary in what they experience and how they cope with that phase; they will not all be horror stories as my sample of interviewees might suggest. Relating what I have was primarily to emphasize that the before-the-beginning phase is a crucial one in the creation of a setting, a phase that cannot be ignored by anyone who wishes to understand the life course of that setting.

Another very practical aspect of that phase—for an undetermined number of charter schools—is that the group creating them has to locate and pay for space in the community. In almost all of these instances the entering cohort of students was or will be relatively small and the per-pupil funds for these schools deemed sufficient only to rent a relatively small space as well as cover costs of salaries, books, materials, computers, etc. After that small, initial cohort in the first year, more students will be enrolled until the full complement of students proposed in the application is reached. Finding space is one thing, finding appropriate, enlargeable space is another thing. Some, not a few, charter schools became aware of these difficulties both before and shortly after they became operational and that has complicated planning and decision making, and has raised anxiety about achievement of goals. Here again I must remind the reader that I am reporting anecdotes others have related to me. Again, unfortunately, we will never know how generally valid these anecdotes are or how these difficulties impacted on the new setting. If anything can be predicted about a new setting, it is that the brute fact of limited resources confronts its creators very early on. And matters are not helped any by the enthusiasm and optimism of the creators, factors which cause them egregiously to underestimate the consequences of limited resources. Their myth of unlimited resources—or the expectation that somehow adequate and appropriate resources will be obtained—is exposed for what it usually is: a myth.

The final factor relevant to the before-the-beginning phase is time. In Connecticut, which created 24 charter schools, the interval between approval of an application and the opening of a school was approximately 6 months. But there is another interval and that is the one between when the creating group begins to meet and when the application is sent off to the state department of education. It is an interval during which personal commitments are made, governance issues are discussed and clarified, educational goals and pedagogy discussed and formulated, community resources identified, criteria for selection of students and personnel formulated, etc. It is not a linear process. Not all members (teachers, parents, other community individuals) may be known to each other; all are assuming unfamiliar roles; there are varying degrees of sophistication about classrooms, pedagogy, finances, educational philosophy and history, and the "psychology" of the age range of the students who will be in the school. Convening such a group is easy; gaining cohesiveness, mutual trust and respect, and other than a superficial understanding of the basic educational issues at stake is far from easy. We know enough about group dynamics to expect that differences in personality, style, status, assertiveness, articulateness, and personal agendas will come into play. Even at this early stage there is someone who is seen as the leader or someone who wants to be seen in that way. The possible scenarios are many and complicated. Undoubtedly there have been groups who never got to the point of agreeing on and sending off an application. That we will never know because no one will ever observe and record the process culminating in an approved application, i.e., how decisions were arrived at, who were most influential in arriving at those decisions, who played relatively passive roles, what disagreements or differences in opinion were glossed over, etc.

In this early phase the participants are actors in and directors of a script which they hope will be produced on the stage of the "real" world. It is a phase in which imagination and fantasy are in the picture, and it is a picture in which reality will be shaped to one's purposes. *As soon as they are told that their plans for a charter school have been approved, their phenomenological world changes; they now must act and deal with the real world on a daily basis; they must now implement the explicit and implicit meanings of their written words; major and minor decisions have to be made; they begin to experience the pressures of time and the real world; their time perspective changes; this phenomenological change is swift and associated with varying levels of anxiety.*

The consequences of these changes are, in part at least, determined by the previous nature and quality of the group's dynamics. They learn quickly that planning a charter school is a different cup of tea than having to begin to implement those plans. And, I must emphasize, when there is the pressure of time and deadlines—pressures from external funding sources as well as internal ones—the consequences may vary from minor to major. It is never without consequences.

Thus far I have talked only about the earliest phases in the life of a charter school. Some readers may have already concluded that in my book I had understated the complexity and problematics of creating a setting in comparison to what I have said in this chapter. I agree with that conclusion. Since I wrote the book in 1972, my personal experience as well as what I have learned about the experience of others have forced me to conclude that the seeds of failure (partial or complete) or success of a new setting were sown in these early phases, and they were sown by internal and external agents. And by external I refer to political and administrative leaders who, with the best of intentions, had not the faintest notion of what is involved in creating a setting, especially one that reflects a radical challenge to the educational status quo. So, for example, charter schools will receive the same per pupil expenditure as regular schools, on the assumption that the worth of a charter school will be judged by whether it can improve educational outcomes without increased funding, i.e., the getting-a-better-bang-for-the-buck mentality. No one is in principle opposed to getting a bigger bang for the buck. But in a truly basic and practical sense the *initial* question is whether the innovative governance, pedagogy, and organization of charter schools will achieve their purposes, improve educational outcomes, and can serve as a basis for further changes in the system. If they can, it will have enormous significance for the existing system from which we get whimpers rather than bangs from the buck. What extra resources should a charter school be given for us to determine their educational superiority and worth? *That* is the important policy question. And when I say extra resources (time and funds) I am not advocating large sums of money and unlimited time, but enough as recognition that charter schools will or may require extra support, initially at least and also because charter schools are on uncharted seas. And, it should go without saying, political leaders were and are quite aware that charter schools will encounter opposition from diverse sources not least of which is the existing system.

In my book I did not sufficiently emphasize how complicated the creation of a setting is or can be. That was largely because there were pitifully few accounts of how new settings come into existence. In terms of published accounts the same can be said today. The charter school movement is a national one because of public dissatisfaction with schools, especially in our many urban areas. As I have said, there is no attempt to study a sample of these ventures with the dispassionate comprehensiveness they deserve. Conducting such studies would be no easy matter, but if we ever want to be able to capitalize on the potentialities of charter schools—not from anecdotes, personal opinion, or the vagaries of memory— we are obliged to conduct such studies. Not to feel so obliged is, in my opinion, *political* irresponsibility (Sarason, 1998). Those studies are not the obligation of those who conceive and bring into existence a charter school; they are activists whose days (and frequently nights and weekends) are taken up with myriads of issues, problems, and meetings which, even if they are so inclined, leave no time for dispassionate observation and description. Precisely because they are passionate people, they should not be expected to be even semi-objective reporters. We should be grateful for what they are trying to do, and we should not expect them to do what they cannot do.

Let us now turn to major variables in the creation of a setting, which are present from its earliest days and loom larger after it comes into operational existence. I refer to leadership, governance, and resources. To give concreteness to the discussion I will use a recent study—the only one I have come across—of five charter schools a year after they started. The study is by Abby R. Weiss (1997) of the Institute for Responsive Education at Boston's Northeastern University. It is entitled *Going it Alone*. I am indebted to her and the Institute for permission to quote from their publication.

The following is from the executive summary at the beginning of the report:

- **There is a high degree of satisfaction among participants.** At each of the charter schools that we visited, there is a high degree of satisfaction among the participants. Students feel that they are being challenged and that they are respected. Parents feel they belong to a larger community and are pleased with the education their children are receiving. Teachers reported a high level of team work among colleagues and flexibility within the charter school setting. Principals spoke highly of their committed staff and the freedom they have to support educational innovation. It was clear from all of our conversations that there is a strong sense of community within these schools and that this enables the schools to survive despite the significant organizational issues that they must address.
- **Governance is a significant barrier.** One such organization issue that is troubling these charter schools is governance; teachers, parents, board members, school founders, and principals cited this as their greatest challenge. Creating a collaborative decision-making structure that is also efficient is causing a great deal of stress at several of these schools. Additional issues that are interfering with the functioning of these schools include the enormous time pressures, the need to create a climate and culture that is consistent with the school's philosophy and conforms to a clear vision, and the demand for improved public relations both within the school and without. All of these issues are compounded by the isolation these schools are encountering both from other charter schools as well as within their local communities.
- **Educational issues need more attention.** Finally, charter school teachers shared with us a belief that educational issues—such as defining student outcomes and developing curricula to move them towards those goals and assessments to measure their progress—need more of their attention. Moreover, teachers expressed the need to focus their school improvement priorities and determine realistic goals for themselves. These educational issues are not being given the attention they need because the schools are weighted down by the more urgent organizational issues.
- **Autonomy creates isolation.** From this research, we have discovered that the autonomy these schools experience generates satisfaction, but also results in a system in which these schools are functioning with little support and assistance. Although charter schools in Massachusetts consider the state to be supportive and proactive, the type of support needed exceeds the role the state envisions for itself. Charter schools need to work more closely with one another, and they need easier access to technical assistance, support, and research to manage some of these organizational dilemmas. In short, they need access to the professional networking opportunities and range of services and information that their colleagues have in both public and independent schools. Without this type of support—

without a more "level playing field"—charter schools will not be able to succeed to the level they might or to fulfill their mission of being laboratories for innovation and school change. (pp. i–ii)

Here are some extracts from the report:

- *Governance.* In several of the schools we visited, governance was highlighted by the school leaders and staff alike as the major barrier to effective implementation of their educational plans.

  At charter schools, every policy, every position, everything the school does for the first time must be created. So decisions, both small and large, need to be made frequently and should be made efficiently. Without a well-defined structure in place for decision-making, the first few months, indeed, the first year, can be extremely difficult.

  The most significant barrier within governance concerns role definitions and decision-making. Many school leaders and teachers are unsure of their job descriptions (one principal had just received his job description after 19 months on the job) and the parameters of their jobs. Which responsibilities are theirs, and which belong to the board? Who should be setting policies? Which policies are to be classroom policies, and which are to be school-wide? How can collaborative decision-making be implemented efficiently?

  Students discussed the difficulties encountered with respect to the governance structure. At one school, where students are very involved in decision-making, one student told us, "I wish they wouldn't make decisions and then ask our opinion of them; I wish they would give us a chance to help make the decisions in the first place." This comment suggests that students are very involved in the governance of the school and feel ownership over the process. At this same school, observation of a governance group which included students and staff showed that student participation and input is taken seriously. But at this school, governance and decision-making is tricky.

  Teachers commented that they feel conflicted about the level of student involvement because it often interferes with their ability to discipline. They respect the students and do not want to undermine their participation in the governance of the school, however they need to make clear to them that the teachers are still the authorities. One teacher said, "I'm not sure what my roles here are. Are students and teachers equal? What rules are negotiable?"

  At another school, one parent, who is also a board member, commented, "Our governance is an untried model. We had no policies in place and no job descriptions. We need to decide who should do what. These roles need to be defined, so that we can start writing policies." (pp. 11–12)

- *School climate and culture.* Another organizational issue, related to governance, found at several of these charter schools is creating a school climate and culture that is based on respect and trust but which also sets appropriate limits for students. These schools are facing a difficult dilemma: they want to create a discipline policy that establishes a stable school environment but that is not so restrictive that it conflicts with the philosophy of the school. Schools are finding this balance difficult to achieve. Especially in those schools in which students are actively involved in governance, teachers are having difficulty drawing the parameters of the roles of the students.

As was already mentioned under governance, the climate and culture issue has two sides. One teacher said, "The culture here is both what works best and worst. Because of the free culture, kids have ownership, and that's great. But they show up late and there are no clear consequences. Even though it is prohibited in our constitution, kids can opt out of doing work."

At a couple of schools, we found a lack of a clear vision. At one school, a teacher commented, "We're still figuring out what we're about. We're trying to be about everything all the time, and we are stretched too thin. We lack a clear vision." At another school, when asked, parents could not tell us what the vision of the school was. Parents said, "We're not there yet," and "We have many visions." We found that without a clear vision, schools have a more difficult time with the decision-making processes and policy-setting. A clear vision allows schools to establish predictable policies, as well as expectations for their community members, all of which flow from this common understanding of what the school is about. (pp. 12–13)

- *Time.* All of the teaching staff and principals that we have met with reported that their work hours are long and intense. Despite the fact that these schools are committed to structuring a great deal of common planning/professional development time into the school day, teachers and school leaders spend a considerable amount of time beyond the school day planning and working together on organizational issues. One teacher told us that his board deliberately hired young teachers because teachers in their early twenties are unlikely to have the familial obligations that would keep them from making the enormous time commitment necessary to their charter school positions. Staff burn-out is a major concern.

  Time is also an issue during the charter planning process. The time it takes to plan a school is significant, and most states do not account for this in their charter application schedule. Several founders told us that they found it difficult to plan the school carefully during the application process, and, as a result, they wrote very broad applications in an effort to please the reviewers. When their applications were accepted, they were forced to try to implement their very ambitious plans. School planners do have (in some states) the option of delaying opening their school for a year after their application is accepted, however, there are limited state funds to support that year of planning. In Massachusetts, the state gives federal money for startup which can be used to delay opening if the school desires. (pp. 13–14)

- *Financial Issues.* There are several pieces to this often-cited barrier to effective implementation. First, several of the school leaders and founders complained that inadequate start-up funding was a difficulty in the early stages of the school development. At most schools, staff could not be hired until shortly before the school opened as there were not enough funds to pay salaries over the summer. In those schools where they were able to hire the teachers sooner, principals reported that this time was indispensable for planning, marketing, and meeting with future students.

  Second, several of the founders cited finding a facility as their number one barrier to implementation. Insufficient start-up money left founders with the difficulty of finding an adequate site that they could afford. Boards and principals were then left with the task of renovating and furnishing space with limited resources.

  At most of the schools we visited, all role groups commented that the facility is inadequate. Because school populations are increasing by at least a grade every year, space that easily accommodated the student population in the first year is quickly outgrown. Therefore, many principals are searching for new space only two years into their program. (p. 14)

- *Public Relations.* Public relations is a very serious issue for charter schools. Charter schools need to reach out to their communities, in order to recruit students, to share resources, and simply to establish a healthy relationship with their neighbors. Several charter schools informed us that their relationship with their surrounding community needs improvement. Communities that house charter schools are often hostile to them because they feel that the charter school takes students and valuable resources away from the non-charter public schools.

  Students and parents reported that they were chastised openly for going to the charter schools. One parent reported that as soon as the teachers learned that she was moving her children to the charter school the next school year, "I was no longer welcome at the school, and that was really hard on my kids." One eighth grade boy was criticized by friends from his previous school for attending a school that was "taking money away from their public school."

  Another major public relations task for the principal is to convince others of the school's merits before there is a program in place. Convincing parents to send their children to a school that is not yet open is difficult, but critical, as the amount of funding a charter school receives depends upon the number of students that attend. Principals reported that, prior to the first year, they invested a great deal of time meeting with parents and students and, where possible, had their school staff available to meet with and plan with the parents and students as well. But until just before the school opened, they were unsure of the exact number of students that would be attending which added stress and pressure to the situation. (p. 15)

- *Isolation.* These educators are creating new schools and are undertaking this monumental task by themselves (by definition, they do not receive district support).

  Charter schools often feel isolated from their communities, and many are not accessing the valuable resources in the community of charter schools. Charter schools could benefit from this interaction in order to address their many common issues while also recognizing and maintaining their core individuality. When we asked principals about their networking with other charter school personnel, they acknowledged that charter schools are not networking in a meaningful way. A few of the school heads meet informally, but for the most part, school leaders report that they are not in conversation with other schools. And a couple of principals did not express much interest in this prospect either. The schools do send a staff person to the occasional conferences or meetings, but these are not regular, and, for the most part, there does not appear to be much opportunity for sharing. (pp. 15–16)

- *The Role of Parents.* Some heads of school, some teachers, and even some parents identified a few barriers they confronted with respect to the nature of the parent involvement in their charter school. Because many charter schools are founded by parents, many cited a difficulty in role definition and role delineation.

  One school in particular had some difficulties with founding parents having an aggrandized view of their own roles with regard to the school's governance. At that school, parents and school leaders commented that it is important for founding parents to separate their personal interests and motives from what is best for all of the students in the school. Parents at that school also noted that some parents attempt to tell teachers how to teach and how to run their classrooms. The school leader and teachers at that school were generally extremely positive about the active participation of parents, however, and the criticisms that were mentioned evidently referred to a very small minority of the parent population.

  From our observations, it is clear that charter schools need to educate their parents about the work they are doing, the vision of the school, and their expectations both for the parents and the students. We found that when parents' expectations of the school and teachers are realistic, teachers referred to the parents as "helpful" and "supportive." When parents are not clear on the school's goals and vision, parents are less helpful and are perceived by the teachers to be more critical. (pp. 16–17)

- *Diversity.* At one of the schools we visited, a student remarked, "the students here are not very diverse. But I don't mind because there are things here that I didn't have at my old school like small classes." This student also spoke about the sense of community that exists at her charter school that she did not find at her previous school.

At another school, with a very mixed population, a young student remarked that many of the students at the school are not used to attending school with children of other races, so there is some tension. Neither teachers nor principals raised any racial issues.

At each school, the principal informed us that the student population does reflect the demographics of the community in which the school is located. The Massachusetts Department of Education states that white students comprise about half of the state-wide charter school population. At every school we visited, the teaching staff looks very much the same— largely white and very young, often with little previous teaching experience. In those schools where the student population is white, the teachers reflect the ethnicity of the student population. However, in those schools where the student population is largely African-American, the teaching staff is still mostly white. (p. 17)

Several things are clear in this report. The first is that the creators, the state department, and the political leadership simply did not appreciate the *predictable* problems the new settings would or may encounter. The creators truly had to go it alone and, as the report indicates, what they wrote in their application were *general* statements of purposes and goals and little or nothing about how they would cope with what I consider to be predictable problems. I have to conclude that political leaders who pushed for charter school legislation, in addition to the state department of education, regarded the creation of a charter school as, so to speak, a piece of cake. They were, to say the least, unhelpful both in the before-the-beginning phase and after. I am not being derogatory when I say the creators were naive, that their initial enthusiasm and optimism, as well as their desire to say what they thought state officials wanted to hear, prevented them from realistically assessing the implications of the venture they were embarking on. Perhaps the most general statement one can make is that no party had anything resembling a conception of what creating a setting entails.

Equally clear in the report is the predictably thorny, frustrating governance issue. Given the diversity of actors involved in creating a setting— varying as they did in experience, status, and much more—governance issues should have been anticipated and, to the extent possible, ways to cope with them should have been discussed candidly and seriously. As I would have predicted, in the before-the-beginning phase that kind of discussion hardly took place, as if governance issues would or could be handled or resolved once the school became operational. But, again as the report indicates, the pressures and problems in the initial year are not conducive to dispassionate, reasoned, candid discussion of governance issues.

The report says nothing about the inevitable relationship between leadership and governance. Indeed, the report surprisingly says nothing about leadership. In my book it is obvious that I regard leadership style (personal and conceptual-intellectual) as a crucial variable. Leaders do and want to put his or her imprimatur on the setting. That is a glimpse of the obvious, as is the statement that there are leaders and there are leaders. There are some charter schools which, in reaction to stultifying leadership and governance of traditional schools, have sought (or said they would seek) to avoid the one overall leader but rather propose a consensus form of governance in which no one person is the leader. Apparently, in none of Weiss' five schools was that consensus form of governance employed.

I do not feel it necessary to indicate how other developmental-organizational issues that Weiss reports were predictable from what I said in the book. Unless I am deluding myself (a possibility), what she reports is what I predicted in several talks I gave long before her publication. That, I hasten to add, does not mean that I regard my conceptualization of the creation of settings as valid in all respects or as comprehensive as it might be. That is why I deem it so unfortunate that charter schools are not being studied and described in the necessary detail and with necessary care in order (1) to learn from the initial cohort of schools, the Model A, what changes should be built into Model B schools, and (2) to have a far better basis than we now have for developing a better conceptualization of the creation of settings.

A final comment on Weiss' study derives from the following:

> Teams of two to three researchers spent one day at each school, visiting classes and governance meetings, touring the facilities, interviewing principals, founders, teachers, parents, and students, and conducting focus groups of students, parents, and teachers. We visited two urban schools, and three suburban, all within one and one half hours of Boston. The five schools represent different grade spans: kindergarten through fifth grade, kindergarten through eighth grade, fifth through eighth grade, sixth through eighth grade, and seventh through ninth grade. (p. 1)

I do not regard, nor does Weiss, spending one day at each school as a basis for drawing conclusions relevant to the longitudinal development of a new setting. But that is all that a private foundation was willing to fund. What surprised me was that a one-day visit allowed her to identify *some* of the most important consequences of a most superficial conception of creating a setting. This is not to say that creating a setting can *ever* proceed smoothly, with no ups and downs, no errors of omission and commission, no unpredictable threats to its viability, no personal or philosophical sources of conflict. Not in this world with our human imperfections. But that does not justify walking into battle with your arms down and your chin up. I say that not only in regard to internal, longitudinal dynamics but also to emphasize that a new setting is surrounded by older settings some of which are far from neutral to the new one. Weiss titled her report *Going it Alone*. The implications of that title are certainly valid as description of the phenomenology of those in the charter schools she visited. But, as she makes clear, from the perspective of some external people and agencies, the charter school was an unwelcome "loner," one they would like to see go away.

For more than a decade before I wrote the book in 1972 my interest in education centered on the rationales for the diverse efforts to improve schools. Beginning in 1965 I predicted that those rationales were seriously, indeed fatally, flawed. With each passing year there was mounting evidence that my prediction had not been an unwarranted indulgence of pessimism. Our educational system is not capable of changing itself. That is why I attached such significance to the beginnings of the charter school movement, which was largely the result of initiatives by state governors and only later endorsed by federal political figures.

A merger here and a merger there are in some ultimate sense less significant for the national welfare than what happens to schools, especially in our urban areas. Precisely because charter schools represent an unprecedented critique of and challenge to the existing system, we should feel obliged to support and study them in the most careful, serious, and dispassionate way. If, as in 1965, I felt compelled to predict what I did, I now have to predict that the superficial conceptual rationale for creating charter schools will give rise to processes of implementation that guarantee that, generally speaking, they will fall far short of the mark. I have no doubt that some charter schools will be success stories. Unfortunately, as things are now we will never know why they succeeded, just as we will not know why those that fell far short of their mark, or completely failed, had the fate they will have. It should be obvious, of course, that when I say "study" I mean taking seriously that charter schools are instances of creating new settings, a process that is as fascinating as it is complex, that begins long before the school opens its doors; that it interrelates individual and group dynamics; that directly and indirectly impacts on and is in turn impacted upon by its community surround; that demands clarity of purpose, means and forums for self-scrutiny, and the wisdom to know the difference between compromise and caving in. Yes, creating a setting that will achieve its goals is a complicated affair. It is not a venture for everyone. It should not be undertaken *only* because one is motivated to do so because he, she, or they have what they consider to be a vision superior or better than those of others. The minimal condition for creating a setting is that you have not underestimated or glossed over the predictable issues and problems that confronts anyone who wants to create a new setting. It is a constant source of amazement to me that so many people who truly have experienced and know the complexities of our social and institutional world forget what they have learned when they undertake the creation of a setting. I consider what I have written about the creation of settings to be glimpses of the obvious. As the reader will undoubtedly attest, the obvious is something we find ourselves re-recognizing again and again.

CHAPTER 7

The Manhattan Project, Charter Schools, and the Creation of Settings

We use the word *create* in different ways on different occasions. When we read a novel we say that it is the creative endeavor of the author, i.e., he or she "dreamed" it up, organized and wrote it. When we visit an art museum or gallery we take for granted that the signature on the painting is that of its creator. When we see a play or a movie, attribution is not so simple. The written script is the creative work of a person, but the script is not the movie. For a script to become a movie or a play requires the creative endeavors of a producer and a director who, so to speak, have to translate that script into a medium of concrete visual imagery and sound. As between producer and director, it is the latter's creativity to which we assign the greatest weight, i.e., he or she brought together a variety of factors and people to create the movie or play. So we say "That is a Howard Hawks movie" or "That is a Billy Wilder movie" or "That is an Orson Welles movie," and we have no doubt who the creator is, although it is by no means rare that conflicts between director and producer about the production are seen by the director as interfering with the creative process; the director sees him- or herself as a singular creative artist and the producer as company or business leader, while the producer may see him or herself as both. There can be conflicts which can mightily dilute the director's pride in the finished work. As viewers we know nothing about such goings on, we may like or dislike the movie and we assign approval or blame to one person: the director, unless those conflicts have been written up in certain mass media. That was never the case with a Charlie Chaplin film because he was author, producer, director, and leading actor. He was *the* creator, no ifs, ands, and buts.

In defining what I meant by creating a setting, I was emphasizing the social-interpersonal factors shaping the process. The idea of a new setting may be that of a single individual, but once he or she takes steps to realize that idea in action, not only does the social-interpersonal come into play but the intellectual-conceptual as well. That is to say, the idea, the vision, the goal has to be intellectually-conceptually clear at the same time that it elicits a positive emotional response leading, hopefully, to commitment. It is characteristic at that point in time, especially if only two people are involved, that issues of leadership stay in the background; the emphasis is on fleshing out the intellectual-conceptual implications of the idea, which can alter the idea in significant ways. Issues of leadership or "ownership" do not arise. When, however, the person with the idea presents it not to one person but to a small group—which is what happens frequently in the case of a charter school—communication and clarification of the idea are more difficult and problematic. At least in my experience, issues of leadership and ownership may not get articulated but arise in the minds of some in that group, e.g., one individual may think it a good idea but does not consider the person who came up with the idea as an appropriate leader, or another person believes that he or she will be able to shape the new setting in ways more congenial to his or her purposes. My point is, I think, obvious: when two or more people get together to create a setting, the chances are nil that there will be no misconceptions, no misunderstandings, no seeds of future problems. Not in this world. Whether any of these *predictable* issues arise and become significantly problematic is another matter, but to proceed as if they will not occur is, to put it mildly, unrealistic. I stress that because my experience and observations forced that conclusion on me. And that is why in discussing charter schools, I am not overly optimistic about what they will accomplish. And among many reasons I put high on the list is a glossing over of issues surrounding leadership and governance, especially in those instances where they have agreed to collective leadership, a term I consider an oxymoron. That explains, only in part, why I consider the Manhattan Project, the name given to the task to develop an atomic bomb during World War II, relevant to my purposes. The Manhattan Project and charter schools are in vastly different worlds of human activity and problem solving but, as I shall try to describe, they are, conceptually speaking, kissing cousins.

Hundreds of books have been written about the Manhattan Project, ranging from the technical-scientific to the personal memoir.[1] For my limited purposes it is sufficient to list the following of the project's features.

---

1. In the many books on the Manhattan Project, I found two most helpful for my purposes: Richard Rhodes' encyclopaedic *The Making of the Atomic Bomb* (1988) and Stephan Grouett's *Manhattan Project* (1968). For reasons that will become clear, my focus is on the Los Alamos part of an engrossing story, and engrossing is an understatement. I suggest that the general reader begin with Grouett's book.

1. The immediate stimulus for the project was a study demonstrating that the atom had been split with an attendant release of energy. On both sides of the Atlantic physicists saw its potential implications for the development of an atomic bomb of unprecedented destructiveness. Such a bomb could decide victory or defeat in the war.

2. Releasing the atom's energy was one thing, harnessing that energy was quite another thing. It was by no means certain how to do it, assuming it could even be done and could be determined quickly enough to be of practical use in the war.

3. Even if it could be harnessed, a more thorny problem was whether that harnessing could be made self-sustaining, i.e., the energies of the split atom would cause other atoms to split in a chain reaction releasing increasing amounts of energy. Could that process be *safely* controlled? Physicists were by no means certain it could be, certainly not in any immediate future. They were dealing with a scientific and engineering process and problem new to them.

4. Different aspects of these problems began to be intensively studied in different university laboratories. These activities were under the aegis of the military. The code name for these different projects was The Manhattan District. Each of these projects had a relatively narrow function. Each in its own way was part of a tooling-up process in regard to a scientific problem which, if overcome, had bearing on the feasibility of an atomic bomb.

5. When it became evident that an atomic bomb might be feasible, it also become evident that to make and test such a bomb would require the creation of an enormous industrial complex of unprecedented scale, in which industrial site A did not know there was a site B, C, etc. Secrecy was paramount. There was every reason to believe that German physicists and the Nazi government had drawn the same conclusions from the splitting of the atom as those in the United States. Because the manufacturing-industrial sites were in different parts of the country, the code name of the project became The Manhattan Project.

6. General Groves was the overall director of the project. Previously he had overseen the building of the Pentagon. He was unfamiliar with the culture of science, and he did not take kindly to what to him were the apparently inefficient, haphazard, informal ways scientists organized themselves and their work. He was a quintessential workaholic who saw himself as having to deal with the "real" world, which he believed scientists did not and could not. One of his junior officers described him as "a sonnofabitch who got things done." That was said with respect and for purposes of praise.

7. It was General Groves who chose Robert Oppenheimer, a highly regarded theoretical physicist, to be the scientific director at Los Alamos, the iso-

    lated New Mexican site chosen for the building and testing of the bomb. Oppenheimer was the scientific director, but there was never any doubt that Groves had final say about everything.

8. If you set out deliberately to choose two people who had to work intimately with each other and yet were as different from each other as day is from night, you could not do better than Oppenheimer and Groves. The ingredients for interminable, interpersonal warfare were all there. It did not work out that way, which is not to say there were no problems or conflicts. They got along amazingly well.

9. It may well be that at no time or place in human history was there such a *working* assemblage of ability, creativity, individualism, ambitiousness, and sheer quirkiness than at Los Alamos. Between the polarity that Oppenheimer and Groves represented, plus the cast of characters who lived and worked together in isolated Los Alamos, the creation of that new setting could be regarded as a disaster whose time had come. Again, it did not work out that way. In terms of its purpose it was successful. And most, if not all, who were there in those years regarded their experience as a kind of intellectual Camelot in which the release of "energy" in one person had a chain reaction in others. And if, as there were, interpersonal conflicts among off-the-scale egos, the energies released by those conflicts were harnessed and controlled.

    At the risk of oversimplification I would suggest there are several factors that enter into an explanation of why Los Alamos is an instance of the successful creation of a setting. The first factor was that every participant knew—in a way that people generally did not know—that Germany possessed the knowledge and capability to make the bomb and if they did so before the Americans, the war was over. (This point was most poignant for the significant number of Los Alamos scientists who were Jewish and/or refugees from countries taken over by Hitler.) Put in another way, if Germany got the bomb first, the accustomed world of science and scientists would vanish, as would the America people knew. Defeating the enemy took precedence over personal ambitions, rugged individualism, personal likes and dislikes, and style of working. At Los Alamos an "agreed-upon purpose" was overarching and a source of control over the excesses of people working at cross purposes. There were no cross purposes. There were, of course, arguments, conflicts of diverse kinds, and controversy but the agreed-upon purpose kept them from being truly disruptive.

    The second factor was that the Manhattan project came close to invalidating the myth of unlimited resources. Practically all that it needed it got because in the first 2 years of the war it was by no means clear that the German-Japanese juggernaut could be stopped. Material resources were not the problem, it was time that was the most precious resource.

The third factor was obvious but it deserves emphasis: The basic scientific issues surrounding the splitting of the atom, harnessing of its energy, and producing a chain reaction had been overcome; the production and testing of an atomic bomb were, so to speak, applied or engineering problems, albeit with scientific implications. If the production of the bomb had its uncertainties, there was no doubt that the basic scientific issues had been incontrovertibly overcome. There was no disagreement whatever on that score.

The fourth factor has two parts. The first concerns the relationship between Oppenheimer and Groves. Organizationally, Oppenheimer was accountable to Groves, and as I have indicated, Groves was a no-nonsense, authoritarian, non-reflective, career-military individual who could and did make quick decisions. And one of those decisions was to choose Oppenheimer; indeed, he chose him over other more world-famous physicists, and he did so even when he was told that Oppenheimer would not receive top security clearance because of his leftist friends and political views. When Groves wanted something or someone, he knew how to get what he wanted. Oppenheimer was given the necessary clearance. When asked why he chose Oppenheimer, Groves said he had never discussed *any* topic with him about which Oppenheimer was not knowledgeable; the one exception being sports. That was said in jest but the fact is that Oppenheimer was a polymath, in and out of physics, and most of the scientists at Los Alamos came to the same conclusion. Oppenheimer was not only a sensitive leader, a respecter of the needs and abilities of others, someone who got the best out of his people, but he could also be decisive when he had to make hard decisions. Initially there was a question about whether he would be cowed by the brilliance and accomplishments of some of the people a number of whom were Nobel laureates, and some younger people who became Nobel laureates. That did present problems of "ego," but Oppenheimer handled them forthrightly and well. He was not a leader on an ego trip; he knew what needed to be done and he didn't allow his personal likes and dislikes, or those of others, to influence his decisions. He got the job done, *his* job. Despite the dramatic ways in which Groves and Oppenheimer differed in personality and style, they both got their jobs done.

The second part of the fourth factor concerns the fact that there were two leaders at Los Alamos, a fact that far more often than not spells trouble ahead. We know more about conflicts between and among other participants at Los Alamos than about the Groves-Oppenheimer conflicts. Each respected the other, each knew he needed the other, and both knew that the stakes were too high to allow any conflict to be disruptive. My guess is they liked each other; it was not a case of tolerating each other.

So what is the relevance of the Manhattan Project for charter schools? I caution myself, as I do the reader, that given the fact that charter schools are in their infancy we do not have for them accounts and descriptions that allow us to compare them in terms of the creation of settings. That I shall endeavor to draw "lessons" from the Manhattan Project for charter schools I justify on the grounds that on the basis of what I have experienced, know, and observed, I have concluded that charter schools will fall far short of their mark. Also, I have no reason to expect that charter schools will ever be written up with that degree of comprehensiveness so as to allow us to understand what happened and why. Put in another way, what follows below is a form of prediction, i.e., identifying factors in the creation of settings which force me to conclude that charter schools will be another well-intentioned, very flawed effort at school reform.

1. From the president on down the Manhattan Project was seen as crucial to the survival of the country. No resources were spared in the effort to determine whether atomic energy could be used to make the bomb. Although the existence of the Manhattan Project was kept from the public for understandable reasons, there is no doubt that the nation would have supported the effort. We are not at war today, but all of our more recent presidents have emphasized that unless we improve our schools (especially our urban ones) American culture, values, social fabric, and social stability will deteriorate. Unlike any time in our national history, the inadequacies of our schools are a source of concern, anxiety, and foreboding. If in World War II the enemy was external, our Achilles heel today is our educational system. What resources should be made available to a charter school? In almost all instances the legislative answer has been that a charter school should receive the same funding as a traditional school. That answer completely bypasses the basic question: What types and level of resources would a charter school require in order to achieve its stated goals? If we know anything about the creation of settings, it is that resources quickly become a major problem. Setting an arbitrary limit to the resources a charter school will receive may serve the obligations of equity and dilute the opposition of traditional schools in a traditional system, but it also may be, as I predict it will, one of the sources of the partial or complete failure of many charter schools. I am not suggesting that we give charter schools a blank check but rather that if a president hails charter schools as a way to improve education—at the same time he says our schools are not accomplishing what they should—should not charter schools be given more resources than the traditional school, especially (as in the case of the Manhattan Project) since charter schools will be sailing on uncharted seas? In World War II the question was not how much will the Manhattan Project

cost, but rather what do we have to do to find out if an atomic bomb is feasible? Presidents, their rhetoric aside, do not ask that question about educational reform. Will charter schools accomplish their goals? Apparently, President Clinton has no doubt that they will. What allows him to ignore the resource issue? When President Franklin Roosevelt gave the go ahead to the Manhattan Project, it was not because he or any of the scientists had no doubts about the success of the effort but rather because its potential was such that we had to support the effort regardless of the level of support it would require. Yes, we were at war and the effort had to be made. Yes, our educational system has been intractable to reform, and charter schools represent the most direct challenge to that system. What if the Manhattan Project failed and we learned later that one of the reasons was that the project was not given the resources it needed and asked for? How would we react? Similarly, how will we react if (as I predict) inadequate resources will be a major factor in the failure of many charter schools to achieve their purposes?

2. In the creation of settings leadership is crucial. When the military chose General Groves, they knew why they were choosing him: a relevant track record, an internally driven man who knew how to drive others, and who understood the military and industrial cultures. It is noteworthy that when he was offered the position, he was not yet a general, he was a colonel, and he said that anyone who would be in that position should be a general because he would have to be dealing with generals who could "pull rank" on a mere colonel. He was made a major general. (Groves really wanted to go overseas, and, I speculate, he may have insisted on the promotion in the hope that the answer would be negative and he would be sent where he wanted to be. In any event, his request says a good deal about his understanding of the military culture. He knew what status-power would be required to get the job done.) In choosing a scientific director he knew it had to be someone who was more than an administrator, someone with the intellectual and professional credentials and personal integrity and self-confidence that would enable him to run herd, so to speak, over scores of talents and egos. On what basis are leaders of charter schools chosen? As best as I have been able to determine, leaders of charter schools are *self-selected*. When an application for a charter school is approved, it is a decision, initially at least, based on a written application. After approval there may be a meeting between the applicant and a representative of the state department of education (it varies from state to state) but that is after the application is approved; the question of leadership does not come up. Self-selection is no basis for leadership, certainly not the sole basis. I am sure there are and will be instances where the self-selected leader has (or will have) what it takes to create and sustain the new setting consistent

with its purposes. But I am equally sure that in most instances that will not be the case.

3. You cannot separate leadership and governance. What sent Groves up a wall was to him the seemingly chaotic, time-consuming, inefficient ways that groups of scientists met, talked, speculated, and mused. One of Oppenheimer's achievements was getting Groves to understand (somewhat) that scientists were a strange breed whose ways of working as individuals or in teams would be hard for others to fathom. There was no "constitution" at Los Alamos detailing governance. In this respect the genius of Oppenheimer inhered in the respect he displayed for what each person or team was doing; his knowledge about what they were doing and why; the quiet, unobtrusive way he observed and conducted himself in the scores of meetings he attended; and the cogency and creativity of his suggestions. Oppenheimer did not pull rank, he did not have to. When he had to make a decision he did so, and because of their respect for him, they came to know that more important than that his heart was in the right place was that his mind was in the right place. At least as I read the record, governance was as much informal as formal. There were seemingly countless opportunities for expression of ideas, and given the cast of characters those opportunities were predictably exploited. The concept of "group think" could not have been derived from observing Los Alamos. What you had there was a culture of learning and doing into which the participants had been socialized long before they arrived at Los Alamos, i.e., whatever "constitution" governed that venue had, for all practical purposes, been written before the project began. A charter school is a different cup of tea. For one thing, the educators involved are faced with the difficult task of forging a new culture, one very different from the traditional one into which they had been socialized. Indeed, they are rebelling against that culture. Nevertheless, they are faced with the thorny task of unlearning the old and learning how to create the new, and that is no easy psychological process. Old "habits" are not easily overcome and acquiring new ones takes time, struggle, motivation, and (yes) courage. It is, as I have emphasized, a feature of the before-the-beginning phase that enthusiasm and optimism cause the creators to underestimate, or not even to recognize, the significance of the problems they will encounter. In the case of the charter school, governance is one of those problems. How will we live and work with each other? By what rules should we be governed? What forums, formal and informal, will be required to insure that ideas, problems, and conflicts get put on the table and openly discussed? What role will participants have in the decision-making process, and when? Those are some of the questions charter school participants have to answer, however provisionally, but for the most part are not addressed, and that, I predict, will be a major factor

in the future story of charter schools. The governance issue is complicated enormously by the fact that charter schools are supposed to involve parents and others in the community in more than cosmetic ways. They are not educators, and the variations among them are far greater than those among the educators in terms of life experience, educational background, status, personal agenda, etc. Potentially those variations are real assets for the schools, but they can also be a source of conflict depending on the clarity of the governance structure and that one of the major purposes of that structure is to forge a sense of community among the participants, *each of whom is in an unfamiliar role in an unfamiliar venture.* That is no easy task. Forging a new culture appropriate to its goals and spirit never is easy, which is why so many new settings become other than intended, frequently regressing to that against which they rebelled. We like to say that we learn from experience. That contains a large kernel of truth. But there is another large kernel of truth: When experience challenges our overlearned ways of thinking and doing and we accept the challenge and seek to change those ways, the struggle to change can be like a magnet pulling us back to the "comforts" of our old ways. That is true both for the individual and the new setting of which he or she is a part.

4. No thought could have been given to the possibility of an atomic bomb until three *basic* problems had been solved, and by solved I mean they did not have to be solved again. They were: that the atom had been split and its energies released, that energy had been harnessed, and that a chain reaction had occurred and had been sustained. Theory and research had produced knowledge about which no one could disagree. The task at Los Alamos was to *apply* that knowledge, a process that was expected to be and indeed was demanding of creativity and ingenuity as well as of the capacity for a self-scrutinizing, self-correcting stance. Initially at least, they were not dealing with problems that had one and only one solution, and what had to be avoided, despite the enormous time pressure, was unduly constricting for any one problem the universe of alternatives to be considered for dealing with it. Time is the most precious of commodities and when you are working under the gun of time, it becomes all too easy to make compromises you will later regret.

Now, in regard to charter schools—indeed in regard to all schools—one has to ask: How much agreement is there in the educational community about the basic problems that have to be solved if educational outcomes are to be significantly improved? Is there one problem which is more basic than the others in that it unlocks the key, so to speak, to other very significant problems? The answer to both questions is that there is no general agreement in the answers to the questions. Perhaps the most frequent answer to the "one basic problem" question is: How children learn, i.e., the nature of the learning process. The fact is that available research in no way unequivocally demonstrates that one answer leads to better results than other answers, which is not to say that there are no differences in their results but rather to emphasize that their results are neither robust nor general enough to produce agreement that one answer and the actions it led to require any fair-minded, knowledgeable person to say that something crucial has been demonstrated which cannot be ignored and counterindicates pursuing other answers any further. We are very, very far from having such an answer. Before the atom was split there were physicists who doubted that it could ever be done, but when the paper demonstrating that it was done was published, doubt evaporated. *I am in no way suggesting that we will ever be able to demonstrate the answer to the learning question with that degree of precision or finality.* In the realm of human affairs that is not possible, but that is no excuse for not seeking the most solid, the most persuasive answer of which we are capable, an answer, I repeat, that would make it difficult for adherents of other answers to continue to think as they do. It is no sin to fall short of the mark, it is sinful not to have a mark, and in regard to the nature of learning in schools, those who determine educational policy and the direction of research have had no mark. The odds are overwhelming that charter schools will provide no answer to the questions I have raised, certainly no answer that will stand up in a court of evidence. They will be unpersuasive because they are not set up to obtain credible evidence, and there will be no basis for making comparisons among them.

How do children learn? That, in my opinion, is not the question we should be asking because it is an oversimplification which obscures three crucial aspects of the problem. The first is, how do you release the intellectual-motivational energies of the child to want to learn? The second is, how do you harness and direct those energies? The third is the equivalent of the "chain reaction": Having released and harnessed those energies, how can it become a self-sustaining feature of the individual's way of learning? Put in another way, what *context* of learning best puts flesh on the bones of those aspects? I sum this up in the phrase "the context of productive learning," a context absent in all but a minuscule number of classrooms, an assertion that includes charter schools.[2] Learning is quintessentially (and obviously) a reflection of social-interpersonal contexts.

---

2. I have written about this in several of my books and whatever summary of their contents I could present here could not be brief and, more important, would distract the reader from what is the purpose of the present book which is, of course, to seek illumination about the creation of settings. The interested reader should consult three of those books: *Letters to a Serious Education President* (1993b), *How Schools Might Be Governed and Why* (1997), and *Political Leadership and Educational Failure* (1998).

The atomic scientists knew what basic problems they had to understand. In regard to the basic problems in school learning, there is no such agreement. Having overcome those problems the atomic scientists had to figure out how to apply that knowledge to the development of a bomb. If the basic problems in education can ever be overcome, application of that knowledge will be far more difficult than developing the bomb because it will require such a drastic change not only in our schools but in all other institutions and agencies which, directly or indirectly, are in relation to schools. It is beyond my purposes to elaborate on what I have said. My purpose has been to indicate why the creation of charter schools will drastically limit what they can persuasively demonstrate, and for that purpose I used the Manhattan Project to make the points I deemed important in as concrete a way as possible. That we need the equivalent of a Manhattan Project in education goes without saying. But let us not overlook that it took a war for survival to initiate the Manhattan Project. Their rhetoric aside, our political leaders at the highest levels seem incapable of taking seriously what steps should be taken to change our schools. In advocating and supporting the creation of charter schools, these political leaders seem unaware that they are indicting our present educational system and its *unproductive* contexts of learning. They are even less aware that the creation of charter schools confronts some basic issues in need of study and clarification. But the way charter schools are being created guarantees that such clarification will not be forthcoming. We have learned many things from the Manhattan Project, not the least of which are most of the ingredients that make for the successful creation of a setting. But what we have learned was only possible because there were people—some who were participants and some who were not—who made it their business to contribute to the descriptive record of what had gone on and why. That kind of record will not be available to us in the case of charter schools. But, then again, the absence of such a record is a feature of the history of educational reform as well as of the history of the creation of settings. The more things change the more they remain the same, or get worse.

CHAPTER 8

Two Ambiguities

There are ambiguities in my definition of the creation of a setting: When two or more people get together over a sustained period of time to achieve agreed-upon goals. The first ambiguity derives from "two or more people," as if to suggest that those people are autonomous, i.e., they are the sole creators, decision makers, or forces. The second ambiguity, deriving from the first, is in the words "agreed-upon goals." It was not until I was well into the writing of the 1972 book that I realized that three of the most important personal experiences which led to my interest in conceptualizing the creation of a setting illustrated the two ambiguities. That is why I inserted the chapter "Buildings as Distractions," because I could identify numerous instances where the creators, far from being autonomous, were in fact representatives of or objects of pressure from diverse groups, official or otherwise, with a vested legitimate interest in the proposed setting. In brief, there were—and this was more than on the surface—at least two major creators, but they were accountable to other leaders with direct or indirect powers to influence the appearance and course of developments of the new setting. Surface appearances aside, there were many leaders, a fact that goes a long way to explaining why these settings fell so short of their mark. It is an empirically valid rule that the more "leaders" who have voice in the before-the-beginning phase of the proposed setting, the more likely that even where the rhetoric of goals remains constant, those goals will later be found to have been undermined by "compromises" in the earliest phases. That rule stems not only from my personal experience but also from that of every architect with whom I have ever talked. For obvious reasons, when a new setting will require a new building (or buildings), architects are in a position—which they consider unenviable—to become aware of the numerous and conflicting positions of the different vested interests. As one noted architect put it to me, "Architects know, at least they say they know, that they serve the interests, hopes, and plans of others who have hired them, but they do not like to be seen as blue print makers who are devoid of ideas and who are expected to exhaust their supply of blue print paper responding to the aesthetic whims and fancies of all those with a stake in the enterprise." If that is the way architects see themselves, it is not unlike what happens between and among the numerous stakeholders, especially when their numbers are not minuscule in the earliest phases of the creation of a setting.

The first personal experience to which I referred began in 1942 when I took my first professional job at the Southbury Training School, a new state institution for mentally retarded individuals in Connecticut. The institution had opened several months earlier. In terms of architecture and educational-residential goals the school deserved the label revolutionary, as I indicated in Chapter 3. For my present purposes I restrict myself to discussing the two ambiguities I have identified. To tell the whole story of the creation and life course of the institution would require a book. There are two features of the story the reader needs to know.

1. Unlike all other comparable institutions, Southbury residents—usually called "children" although their ages ranged from 6 to over 40 years of age—were not going to be warehoused in large, impersonal, congregate buildings. There would be small cottages which would have their own kitchen, dining room, and cottage "parents."
2. Again unlike all other comparable institutions, Southbury would not be medical in orientation but rather educational. This was expressed in terms of a "revolving door" policy: Residents would come in, receive an individually tailored educational or vocational program, and then return to family and community. The home-like features of cottage living was intended to minimize the usual chasm between institutional and family-community living.

It is fair to say that the concept of Southbury—its architecture, educational rationale, and goals—was formulated by (a) as prestigious, courageous, and imaginative a board of trustees as has ever been assembled and (b) its major consultant who was an educator (and frustrated, amateur architect) became the first superintendent over the explicit opposition of the medical community, the medical superintendent of the heretofore only institution for the mentally retarded, which had been built in the nineteenth century, and more than a few members of the legislature. Indeed, *Mister* Roselle became the first superintendent only after the board of trustees said they would resign en masse if the legislature did not confirm their nominee. The before-the-beginning phase of Southbury was not all sweetness and light. There were clouds on the horizon.

Consistent with "agreed-upon goals" you would expect that the institution would not be built in the middle of Connecticut's rural nowhere, i.e., no public transportation, away from population centers containing many economically poor families whose children would become residents and who did not have cars. (The planning for Southbury took place during the Great Depression.)

How did this come about? As best as I could determine at the time from diverse sources, the legislative representative for the Southbury electoral district insisted on locating the institution there as the price for his support in gaining legislative approval. He was a major force in the legislature, an opponent of the governor who was from the other political party who had spearheaded the movement for a new institution. In any event, whatever the context in which that decision was made, it was a decision inimical to achieving agreed-upon goals.

Then there was the decision for the new and older institution jointly to have the same social service department housed in the state capital, miles away from both institutions. That was not the intent of the Southbury board who did not have high regard for the person who would continue to head up the department after the decades she had been in the position. I was told that the medical superintendent of the older institution was a force behind that position because he had such misgivings about Southbury's rationale which implicitly was an argument against the kind of institution he had long directed. From my personal experience with him I can say that he was understandably envious of the resources Southbury had and fearful of dilution of his political-professional clout in the legislature (of a small state). But the strength of his envy paled before his contempt for Southbury's non-medical, "revolving door" rationale. And that contempt was shared by "his" social worker who became director of the joint social service department, largely through his machinations and over the reservations of the Southbury board. The reason her appointment was so fateful can be gleaned by the following statements she would make at case conferences:

1. No resident should be returned to the community before he or she was 18 years of age and/or had been in the institution for at least 10 years. (At that time admission to and release from Southbury was through the probate court, i.e., the resident was a ward of the state, the family had no legal standing.)
2. It is best for male residents that their community placement be on a farm. For females it is best if they are placed as maids in a private home.

The formation of a joint social service department and the appointment of Ms. X were on a collision course with Southbury's "agreed-upon purposes," and those collisions were frequent.

So who created Southbury? As I said in my 1972 book and should have said with greater emphasis, in the earliest phases of the creation of settings one should distinguish between those with "official" responsibility to create the setting and those, whose numbers are not minuscule, who by virtue of interest or power or status seek to influence what that setting will be like. In brief, there are creators who are leaders, and there are leaders who seek to influence creators. I am not suggesting that the influence of the latter is always disruptive or subversive and that when it is, it is not because of the shortsightedness or maladaptiveness of the creators who, so eager and enthusiastic about creating the setting, are rendered insensitive, as one person put it, to "who is in the inter-institutional or inter-agency woodwork." We simply do not have the kinds of comprehensive accounts to allow us to conclude in any one instance whether the influence was positive or negative and why. Of one thing I have become certain: Creators of settings have to force themselves to identify who may be in the woodwork, and to figure out strategies for dealing with them in ways that do not undercut the proposed setting's purposes at the same time that you gain their support or dilute their opposition or gain new ideas. From a purely psychological standpoint the creators of settings gloss over these early phases because of the pressures of time, pressure stemming from internally or externally set deadlines, or an unwillingness to spend what to the creators is a great deal of time.

Let me now turn to the last opportunity I had personally to observe the creation of a new setting, which I introduced in Chapter 3. This experience is quite relevant to the ambiguities "two or more people" and "agreed-upon purposes." The Yale School of Management welcomed its first students in 1970. That Yale did not have a "business" school reflected some longstanding attitudes in the faculty, and at Yale the power, formal and informal, of the faculty is considerable. Neither a president nor the "Yale Corporation" will make important academic decisions of any kind in the face of strongly articulated opposition from the faculty. For example, a recent president made proposals eliminating a department, reducing faculty size, downsizing and practically putting one department out of existence that produced a rebellion among the faculty, an open confrontation with the president, and essentially a vote of no confidence. The president subsequently resigned. From time to time over the decades proposals for a business school were floated but went nowhere, even though so many leaders in business, industry, and finance were and are Yale alumni, not a small number of whom called for the creation of a business school. In the 1960s—and in response to what was happening in that turbulent decade—approval was given to the creation of the Institution for Social and Policy Studies (ISPS) which would have three centers: one on the City, one on Education, and one on Management. None of the centers had the standing and prerogatives of a department; faculty members who chose to affiliate with a center had his or her primary appointment and obligations in an existing department. There was a department of Administrative Sciences, most of whose members had long voiced their opinion that Yale needed a business school, and they viewed a center as less than an anemic gesture to their view as well as to that of alumni.

I said earlier that at Yale the faculty has a good deal of power. That is also the case for departments which see any program and setting not under the direct control of an established department as an alien body. ISPS, essentially a paper organization, was neither fish nor fowl, and although departments went along with the creation of ISPS, they predictably did little to make it intellectually viable. The Center on Management, again predictably, was the first to become a source of conflict as it became clear that it could not serve the purposes of a respectable and respected program meeting the research and training needs of the American private sector. This, it should be noted, was at a time when Yale alumni in that sector concluded that the university (its students and faculty) was no source of moral and intellectual support for a private sector which was being pilloried on all sides as a major cause of society's ills.

What happened next is more than cloudy, but some aspects were revealed to me by John Perry Miller: The first director of ISPS, a professor of economics, former dean of the graduate school, and with more connections to Yale alumni than anyone else I knew in my 45 years at Yale. He *understood* Yale as no other faculty member did. He was a decent, likeable man who had long been convinced that Yale needed a business school, not only because Yale had loyal alumni who wanted it but also because he believed that Yale could create a school which in important ways would be intellectually and academically superior to the usual business school. Essentially he exercised leadership and his connections to major figures of the Yale Corporation to have that body create such a school. The Center on Management disappeared and the planning for the new school started.

I was a member of the committee to choose the dean of the new school whose distinctive purpose would be the admission and training of students approximately half of whom had a major interest in private sector organizations and the other half interested in a career in the public and non-profit sector. That is to say, Yale was not going to have a school preparing students only for the business community. I was asked to be on the committee because the courses I taught were directly relevant to public institutions, agencies, and public schools. I had no intention of switching my appointment from psychology to the new school. Because the new school would have students with interests similar to mine, and who also had previously started careers in the "real" world, I was wholeheartedly in favor of the proclaimed purposes of the new school. By far the most decisive reason I was happy to be on the committee was the opportunity it would provide to observe the creation of a new setting. I say observe rather than participate to emphasize that I believed as a matter of organizational principle that those who will have full time responsibility for the school should make the most important decisions, e.g., choosing a dean, adding faculty, developing a curriculum. I participated in all discussions but not with the passion and perseverance that (some say) are characteristics of mine.

The fact is that even if I had had more of an inclination to participate, it was diluted in strength in the meetings. Over an entire academic year the committee invited more than a half dozen candidates for the position of dean to visit Yale for two to three days during which he or she talked with committee members and administrators at the highest level. And then there was a long post mortem after each visit.

The long and short of it is that the members of the committee, almost all of whom had a vital stake in the new school, could not reach anything remotely resembling consensus on any candidate. More than that, the level of mutual trust and respect among the members was, to indulge understatement, unimpressive. And those meetings revealed diverse and conflicting opinions about the school's purposes. As director, John Perry Miller chaired the meetings but he, like me, would not be in the new school, and he saw his task as helping the committee to complete its mission. It is fair to say that it was a semi-leaderless group. There was no leader-creator who chose his own core group and took full responsibility for all that happened. It was all too obvious that if and when a dean was appointed, he or she not only would have no core group but rather a conflict-ridden one. Henry Kissinger once said that the reason conflicts in the university were so stormy and disruptive was that there is so little at stake. In the instance I am describing that was not the case. The stakes were high. Creating a new school at Yale sends a message that is heard far beyond its physical setting, e.g., alumni world wide.

If I had any reservations about being other than an observer, they were dispelled by those meetings. Yes, I took satisfaction that what I had written about the creation of settings was again being confirmed. But it was no source of pleasure.

Given that an opening date for the new school had been set, choosing a dean became crucially important. It was, I think, John Perry Miller, who early on concluded that no nominee for the position could come from the faculty committee. And given his close ties to the president and the Corporation he must have recommended to them that they would have to exercise the written power of their role in governance to appoint a dean of their choosing. And, so, later in that year they announced the appointment of William Donaldson: a Yale alumnus, a Harvard M.B.A., a well known Wall Street broker, financier and venture capitalist, with no administrative experience in academia. He had no doctorate, no academic teaching experience, and had never conducted research. That the appointment was greeted with dismay is truly to indulge understatement. Donaldson was a likeable, bright, decent, hard-working individual who gave his all to opening the new school and directing it for several years. Even faculty who disparaged him and his appointment later agreed (i.e., after he had left) that *at least* he had gotten the school to open and *that* was no small feat.

It is beyond my present purposes to describe the *sturm and drang* of those early years, which was no less than a playing out of the conflicts so evident in the before-the-beginning phase and no less evident after Donaldson left the scene. But there was one other feature of that phase that deserves emphasis here because it concerns "agreed-upon purposes."

I also served on the committee to develop the curriculum for the new school. I agreed to serve because I wanted to do what I could to have the curriculum seriously to reflect one of the distinctive purposes of the new school: to prepare students for careers in the public, non-profit sectors. And to me that meant, among other things, the field of education. To my knowledge there is no business school in the country that has a faculty member (let alone a program) who studies and understands schools in terms of their history, culture, organization, governance, professional issues, and criteria for evaluation and improvement. Those kinds of studies are the stock-in-trade of business school faculty in regard to private sector organizations. Even though public education is *very* big business, it is of no interest to business school faculty. Given the distinctive purpose of the new school I sought to have the curriculum reflect it in terms of courses, field experience, and selection of faculty. I would be less than honest if I said that I expected to have an influence. From what I have already described I had already concluded that turf battles would be the order of the day; you did not have to be a sage to make that prediction. The details of those battles need not be described here. All that needs to be said is that token gestures to the importance of the public sector were made and I left the scene of those meetings. "Agreed-upon purposes" succumbed to tradition cloaked in the language of innovation. The subsequent history of the new school has reflected in a very direct way all of the errors of commission and omission I describe in my book. It has been an unhappy place.

A third personal experience mentioned in Chapter 3 illustrates the two ambiguities. I came to Yale in 1945 through an appointment in the Institute of Human Relations (IHR) which had been created 15 years before—with a good deal of national fanfare and a lot of Rockefeller money—to demonstrate that bringing together in one place leading representatives of each of the social sciences, including psychiatry and child development, would mightily contribute to understanding human behavior. Given the individuals Yale attracted, IHR might deservedly have been called the Hall of Stars. IHR was to be a centripetal intellectual-research setting, not one of independent individuals concerned only with their own interests and academic domain. By the time I came to Yale that purpose had long been forgotten; it was a collection of fiefdoms. Stories abounded about how this had come to pass. One factor was that the idea for IHR had been developed by three people: Robert Hutchins, the very young Dean of the Yale Law School; Alfred Winternitz, Dean of the Yale Medical School; and Yale's President Angell, the first Yale president who was not an alumnus. They developed the idea, secured the funding, attracted a number of stars but then quickly delegated as leader someone who had few if any academic credentials and whom no one would call a leader. Another factor was that collecting stars each of whom tended to see himself as a sun around whom stars circulated was an invitation to disaster because it was assumed that they would be reasonable people who would adapt to the major purpose of IHR even though they had never previously been required to make such an adaptation, i.e., they had become stars precisely because of their rugged individualism. And that factor interacted with the fact that for all practical purposes there was no leader. The creators were leaders, the person they appointed as director was not. The final factor was that the Yale faculty did not want IHR because it was not under departmental control, which, of course, was the kind of turf mentality which to the three creators of IHR required that it come into existence, not only for Yale's sake but for higher education in general. Departmental boundaries in the university were and are not porous.

If no one has seen fit to write up in appropriate detail the creation and life course of IHR and its major purpose—it did not miss the mark, it fell far short of it—that is not true for the creation and demise of Yale's graduate Department of Education which was studied by Cherniss (1972). His doctoral dissertation was based on what I had learned about the creation of settings. The reader who reads his large volume will see obvious similarities to what I have recounted in my discussion of IHR and Yale's School of Management. In two instructive respects the education department's story differs. In terms of "agreed-upon goals" it met its goals rather well: Over its quarter of a century or so of existence it did turn out far more than a few doctoral students who were research trained and who assumed major positions in universities and in other arenas of education. This despite the fact that the first chairman of the department had not the foggiest notion of the culture of universities in general and Yale in particular. He played into every prejudice that the Yale faculty at the time held. And that is the second respect in which that department's story differs from the other; the difference is a matter of degree but what a degree! To the Yale faculty the creation of the department was an abomination, the beginning of a malignancy that could undermine the health of the university. Not long after World War II a Yale president, who in his speeches and writings, made no bones about his disdain for educators and public schools, eliminated the department. His unilateral action was greeted with enthusiasm by the Yale faculty. The malignancy was extirpated.[1]

I did not write this chapter to pick on Yale to which I have much to be grateful. No university does better than Yale in taking seriously its "agreed-upon purpose": to create the conditions which allows its *individual* faculty members to pursue their scholarly and research interests. Yale is tailor made for individuals. When it comes to creating new settings which will require intimate and serious collaboration-cooperation among its members, it blithely glosses over the predictable problems that will be encountered, the most thorny of which derive from rugged individualism. I have been part of academia for more than half a century, enough to be able to say that the examples I have taken from my decades at Yale have their counterparts in other comparable universities.

It may seem strange that a chapter devoted to two ambiguities in the definition of a new setting should end with a discussion of the Metropolitan Opera House in Lincoln Center. But, as I shall suggest, that opera house says something important about ambiguities of leadership and taking agreed-upon goals seriously.

The Metropolitan Opera House was not created by one person but by a relatively large number of people who by virtue of wealth, or political connections, or proven business acumen, or publicly acclaimed public service had the responsibility to develop Lincoln Center in which the Met would be one part. In other words, the Met was not independent in the sense that it could make its own decisions without consideration of the Lincoln Center authority. No one has written in any detail about the earliest phase of the planning for and decisions about Lincoln Center, but it is safe to assume that although there was no dominant leader, not all who participated had equal influence or power in decisions. We simply do not know the interpersonal-social-professional contexts from which important decisions emerged. One thing is certain: the musical community, however defined, was the opposite of overrepresented in those early phases.

We can also assume in the case of the Met that there was agreement that its agreed-upon purpose was to stage opera that delighted the eye and

---

1. It was the same president who allowed IHR to go out of existence by taking no initiative to secure continued funding.

the ear. From the standpoint of the aesthetics of the architecture I, at least, and I am not alone here, revel in its splendor; it readies me for and transports me to the world of musical drama. But, as I quickly learned on the first of many visits, the Met is a cavernous, humongous "house," probably the largest of its kind in the world, where at least half of 3,800 people in the audience is one to two blocks distant from the stage; and in the highest balcony it is more like three blocks. I have sat in all levels of the Met, and occasionally paid an immoral amount of money to sit in the tenth row center of the orchestra, and that is why I had to conclude that for at least half of the audience the purpose of the Met is hardly achieved. What I am saying here was discussed by Bernard Holland, music critic of the *New York Times*, in the Arts and Leisure section for Sunday, July 20, 1997, in an article titled "A Music Mecca Loved but Reluctantly." He points out that size not only presents problems for the audience but for singers as well, some of whom simply do not have a strong enough voice to be heard in the Met's house. The following makes the point:

> I remember seven years ago, at the Opera Theater of St. Louis, a young tenor named Stanford Olsen singing Donizetti exquisitely before a sold-out audience of 950 at the Loretto-Hilton Theater. Mr. Olsen's subsequent career at the Met has been less happy. Four times bigger, the New York house not only smothered his singing but may have damaged his voice as well.

Mr. Holland points out that other halls in Lincoln Center are subject to the same criticisms.

Why is the Met so big? The usual answer is the economic one: The Met has little or no public subsidy; it must sell tickets, a lot of tickets, to survive and to be able to attract the best native singers and those from the European opera houses.

I can assure the reader that I am quite aware of the brute fact that resources are *not* unlimited. Indeed, in the book I emphasize how all too frequently the creators of a setting do not seriously take that fact into account; they proceed as if they believed in the myth of unlimited resources. The Met did have a serious economic problem, and I understand why the sponsors felt compelled to make it as big as it is. What I do not know is whether they were aware that they were undercutting their "agreed-upon purpose?" That raises another question: How seriously did the different leaders examine the universe of alternatives available to them in light of their stated purpose? If I have learned anything about the creation of settings, it is how hard it is for the leaders-creators to change their mindset about what they envision the setting should be. It would be egregious hubris on my part to attempt to list the universe of alternatives the Met (and Lincoln Center) leaders-creators might have explored. That there was such a universe I have no doubt. I would be surprised if it can be demonstrated that they seriously explored that universe in light of their goal. The answer to my question is contained in the before-the-beginning phase for which of course there is today no written account. What probably happened was that as they dealt with the economic problem *as they defined it*, they lost sight of their stated goal. Put in another way, their goal became economic survival, and that is why I agree with the title of Mr. Holland's article "A Music Mecca Loved But Reluctantly." The Met and Lincoln Center fell short of their mark but not that far short to warrant anything resembling condemnation. Let's just say it warrants ambivalence, and in the arena of the creation of settings that is more than one would have expected.

CHAPTER 9

A New High School

I had the opportunity to spend a day interviewing four people crucial to the creation of a new high school in Providence, Rhode Island. (The meeting took place in August 1997.) The four people were Peter McWalters, Charles Mojkowski, Elliot Washor, and Dennis Littky. A month before I had spent a day meeting with all teachers (N = 4) and staff (N = 7). The school, which had just finished its first year, had 52 students, and would double in students and teachers in the next year. The 52 students were a *total* sample of all who sought entry after a promotional effort to elicit interest in all middle school students in Providence, i.e., essentially, there were no selection criteria. It was hoped that at least 50 students would want to come and when 52 applied, they were all accepted. They were predominantly Black or Hispanic and with few exceptions were at least 2 years behind grade level. Thirty percent of parents could speak no or hardly any English.

I had come to know Dennis Littky 25 years ago when he was principal of the Shoreham-Wading River middle school on Long Island. I visited that school several times and have described one of its programs in my book *You Are Thinking of Teaching?* (1993c). What Littky accomplished there could be attributed to the fact that the school was in an affluent community with highly educated parents supportive of educational innovations. Several years later he became principal of a high school in a relatively poor, working class community in Winchester, New Hampshire. What he accomplished there can be found in two places. The first is *Doc: The Story of Dennis Littky and His Fight for a Better School*, a book written by Susan Kammeraad-Campbell (1989). The second is a 2-hour movie (*A Town Torn Apart*) based on the book and nationally televised by NBC on November 30, 1992. The book is engrossing. The movie I found absolutely stirring. Knowing Littky as well and as long as I do, and what TV movies do to truth, I was prepared for the movie to contain numerous distortions and irrelevances and, like too many classrooms, to make the interesting uninteresting. It is a superb film demonstrating what a principal *and* teachers can do to undo self-fulfilling prophecies.

So when Dennis told me that he may have the opportunity to spearhead the creation of a new high school I had ambivalent reactions. One part of the ambivalence stemmed from the fact that he had demonstrated that he could take a traditional school and transform it, which is not the same cup of tea as creating a new school. He is a charismatic person who can give one, initially at least, the impression of a wild-eyed visionary who lives in a world of utopian dreams, a social radical who challenges the status quo only because it is the status quo. Some people "write him off" immediately, not only because of a first impression but also because his conception of productive education is a critique of their conceptions. Most educators cannot envision themselves in "his" type of school. I feared that he was taking on a task the difficulty of which he was underestimating and for which his personality style could be a significant handicap. The other part of my ambivalence was that few educators have his "street smarts," passion, courage, and educational wisdom. Therefore, if you bet against him successfully doing what he set out to do, you are likely to lose the bet. Also, Eliot Washor, his longstanding friend and colleague, an unusual twosome, is a leavening influence on what Dennis thinks and does.

The story begins several years earlier when the business community expressed its utter dissatisfaction with the Rhode Island vocational schools, a dissatisfaction felt by those in the educational community as well as the public at large. Those schools were less than inadequate. A respected vocational educator in the state department was asked to prepare a report on what should be done. That person was Charles Mojkowski. His experience had already forced him to conclude that it was a mistake, theoretically and practically, to consider the problem and goals of vocational education apart from those of high schools, i.e., what made the high school experience so arid, abstract, and uninteresting was its divorce from societal experience and context and that was too frequently the case with vocational programs. Learning lacking a personally and socially meaningful context extinguished interest and obscured the practical significances of learning. Although his charge was to indicate what should be done about vocational education, he wrote a report which, although it did not say so explicitly, could justify the creation of a revitalized high school in which vocational education was an integral part of *all* education. Charles knew that to demonstrate that point of view could not be done in an existing high school.

Three years later the state sought a new commissioner of education and chose Peter McWalters, with the implicit mandate to change and improve education in the state. Soon after that the legislature passed and the governor approved a $29-million bond issue to build a new high school in Providence which would have a percolating impact on other high schools in the state. McWalters knew Charles, had read the report, and agreed completely with his thinking about the relation of *school* learning to hands-on *work experience* in the community. McWalters is the most unusual commissioner I have ever met. He knew that his own department was part of the problem, but at the same time he did not see its members as villains but rather as well-meaning people who were unwitting victims of their experience and socialization in the field. Nevertheless, he knew he had to protect and insulate any new and innovative school from the more innovation-killing rules and regulations of his department. He also knew that any truly innovative school would meet opposition and criticism from the educational community and the teachers union. McWalters had been superintendent in Rochester (New York), and he knew first hand the unhappy life course of educational reform efforts. And, of course, he knew that the success of the new venture depended to a great extent on finding and attracting a new principal whose views explicitly coincided with his and, no less important, had the imagination, courage, and energy that point of view demanded. Just as McWalters did not see himself as someone who sat in his office and "made policy," he did not see the new principal as someone who "administered."

Not long after McWalters became commissioner Dennis Littky had left New Hampshire to become a senior fellow at the newly created Annenberg Institute at Brown University in Providence. As senior fellow Dennis could do whatever he wanted. He and McWalters began to meet, and it was obvious to both that Dennis's ideas, hopes, and dreams stood a chance of being realized in the new school. He accepted the position in the summer of 1995.

Since this is a chapter and not a book, I cannot go into detail about many things that occurred both before Dennis was appointed and all that happened in the planning year leading up to the opening of the school in temporary quarters in September 1996. Having spent only one day with the four major participants, I do not know all the details. But I know enough to say that Littky and McWalters were able, in very creative ways, to parlay the *possibility* of external support to get the state to release funds for a planning year. In addition, both (especially McWalters) used their networks in the political and business arenas to gain support, material and otherwise. They knew their sources of resistance, but they mounted a public information campaign that very much muted (but did not extinguish) the articulation of that resistance. That campaign involved newspapers, radio, and TV. A full report would contain details that would shed light on other important actions and occurrences relevant to the significance of the before-the-beginning phase, e.g., the selection of teachers (mostly young because experienced teachers expressed no interest), workshops for teachers, meeting with parents of incoming students, work sites for internships, and a temporary site for the school.

In March 1996 the decision was made to open the school the following September. That decision was not made because anyone thought that planning had resolved all issues of practical import but rather because a good deal of public support had been generated which would be squandered if the opening would be postponed for another school year. They knew they were starting with a "model" that would be altered by experience. And by altered they in no way meant departures from the basic rationale but rather improvements for its realization. Here, in brief, is the rationale:

1. A teacher would be responsible for 10 students in a one-on-one way, *the opposite of the imagery of a teacher teaching a group.*
2. The program for any student would be discussed and forged at meetings consisting of the student, his or her parents, and the teacher. Following those initial meetings there would be others during the year, at least four such meetings or more depending on the student's needs, progress, and problems.
3. The responsibility of the teacher was to obtain and coordinate whatever resources were necessary for the student's individualized academic and vocational program. The teacher, of course, could meet many of the student's needs, but it was not realistic to expect that he or she could meet all of them; therefore, the teacher had to be a locator of resources (internal or external) and a coordinator of them.
4. In the first year of the school a student would spend a minimum of one day a week in a work setting of his or her choice. Once a student indicated an area of interest, the teacher would provide the student with information about relevant settings which had indicated a willingness to consider having a student. *It was the student's responsibility to contact that setting, make an appointment for an interview, and prepare for it.* As indicated above, the student's parents participated in the decision, had to approve, and implicitly accept responsibility to support the student in the experience. Parents had responsibilities; they were not passive, uninformed observers.
5. Students are required to organize and write up what they have read about, learned, and did in connection with their placement and any other project (e.g., academic) relevant to their individualized programs. Those writings are discussed as are ways of improving them, the student does a second draft, and there may be several. The final version is at some point publicly presented with parents and invited guests in attendance. For each student there is a file containing these reports which are considered public documents, i.e., anyone internal or external to the school can ask and study the file of any student.

Those are the bare bones of the rationale, without any flesh. Several things are demonstrable from the first year of the school. Parental attendance and involvement have been near total, if only (I assume) because it was the first time in their lives they were treated with respect, given responsibility. They were not objects of the *noblesse oblige* stance; they had a role to play and it was neither superficial and ritualistic. The attendance rate for the students was extraordinarily high by ordinary standards, let alone in comparison with their previous attendance records. They exhibited little or no behavior or motivational problems. They worked and thought hard.

At the end of the school's first year there was a "celebration." At each table there were one or two students, their parents, and one or more members from the business, political, and educational community. Each student had the opportunity to present to everyone at the celebration an account of their year: what they did and learned, giving concrete examples (their reports). The event ran 3 hours. Littky and Warshor were fearful that some of the invited guests had found the evening too long and tiresome and expressed an apology to some of them. Without exception they replied that it was one of the most inspiring evenings they had had in a long time. One business executive said, "If it had gone on another 3 hours I would have gladly stayed." The final event of the evening was a series of graphic presentations on a TV screen. (Littky and especially Warshor are creative exploiters of television, having years before started a closed circuit TV program involving scores of schools around the country.) They presented data, including test data, indicating what students had accomplished.

At one point during my interview with Dennis I asked, "Was there a problem or problems in this first year that was unpredictable, truly surprised you?" Dennis replied, "I vastly underestimated how hard it is for teachers—and our teachers are young and relatively inexperienced—to give up the idea that their job was to teach groups or classes of students. Even though we had emphasized our commitment to the one-on-one approach, they would, especially in the first month or so fall back on teaching in groups. It was hard for them." That reply is not unrelated to something he said later: Essentially, to direct the new school, to play the necessarily major role in keeping participants ever vigilant about agreed-upon purposes, is so time consuming and complex as to run the risk of being unable to do justice to other, very practical issues, e.g., enlarging and sustaining diverse constituencies necessary for the community's support of such a school. At least he was able to express his concern. How he will handle the problem next year when the student and teacher population doubles I do not know.

It is not my intention to pass *any* definitive judgment on this new setting. My overarching purpose is to try to understand and answer this question: Why has this setting not been marked by the divisive, disruptive issues surrounding governance, leadership, and goals, as is so often the case? I should also add "resources" because there is no new school building, there are restrictions on when and how the money from the bond issue can be spent, and it was apparent before the planning year that the state would or could not provide resources that would make a planning year a productive one. Here are the ingredients of my answer.

1. The creators of the setting had over the years survived in their battles for school reform. They were seasoned veterans. They were highly knowledgeable about and sensitive to the *predictable* problems. They did not allow their enthusiasm to minimize or gloss over those problems. They also knew that what happens in the before-the-beginning phase will be fateful for what happens once it opens its doors. Their street smarts extended to more than the culture of schools and the wider educational community. Those street smarts extended to the political system, the business community, and to the larger community and general public. To put it succinctly, if not felicitously, they knew the game and the score. In the best sense of the word they were astute politicians.

2. There were two leaders, Littky and McWalters. The latter was the equivalent of General Groves, and the former the equivalent of Robert Oppenheimer in terms of status and power. They are very different kinds of people or personalities. As in the case of the Manhattan Project, McWalters chose Littky because he had no doubt that as the day-to-day director he would get the job done, even though he knew that Littky was not one to suffer fools gladly, let alone easily. Littky admired and respected McWalters without whose deep support he knew the project was doomed. Before he took the position he had concluded that McWalters was no nitpicking, rule-obsessed, don't-rock-the-boat bureaucrat concerned only with protecting his office. McWalters would, Dennis concluded, be supportive, not intrusive, candid and forthright, not devious. This is not to say that they saw eye-to-eye about everything, but that they do not allow a disagreement to fester, i.e., somehow they work things out.

3. As I have indicated, the agreed-upon goals of a new setting have a way of being reinterpreted or misinterpreted by different participants in the before-the-beginning phase, especially as opening day approaches followed by the realities of day-to-day implementation. That changes will be required goes without saying, but there are changes and there are changes, i.e., some changes do not affect goals, others may or do. Whether it is one or the other type of change, whether the difference between the two is recognized or not, is largely determined by the degree of stress being experienced by the participants—and those early months *are* stressful. In the

case of the Providence project Littky and Warshor have been unusually vigilant in examining any suggested change in terms of goals, which is one of the reasons Littky realizes that that degree of vigilance (and the time it takes) will somehow have to be maintained when the number of teachers and students double next year. In the day I spent with the teachers—where my sole task was to try to be helpful in their personal writeups of the first year—I was impressed by the lack of even a hint of disagreement about goals. There is one goal held with passion by the creators: The new school should be a vehicle by which other schools in Rhode Island will change. No action along these lines have been taken; it is not an issue in their phenomenological present, it is an issue they will deal with later. I expressed the opinion that later is too late, the kind of influence they want to have has to begin now, however small such steps may be. At least in regard to educational reform, disseminating written results, however, impressive, does not hold a candle to some degree of personal observation and involvement. It is a knotty problem.

If I had to put in one sentence the answer to why this truly innovative school is unlike any other new school I observed or know about, it would go like this: The creators were crystal clear about what they wanted to achieve, what the important problems would be, the different ways they could overcome them or dilute their force, the crucial significance of developing diverse kinds of supportive networks and constituencies, the bedrock importance of sincerely involving parents, and that vigilance about values and goals has to be constant and never ending because it is the price paid for the opportunity to remain free from stifling tradition.

The creators are activists, not researchers. Unfortunately, they did not see fit and do not have the funds to get somebody capable of doing a developmental ethnography on the basis of which conclusions can be reasonably drawn about how and why the setting came into existence and the criteria by which its accomplishments and deficiencies should be assessed. It would be a shame if such an account never gets written, leaving us with anecdotes, opinions, and personal testimony deriving from personal friendships (as mine with Dennis and Elliot), testimony that may be largely valid but hardly of a caliber required by the court of evidence. When it comes to educational reform it is, again unfortunately, the case that we come to conclusions more on anecdotes, opinion, and personal testimony than anything else.

Finally, it is relevant here to mention two papers I received last week from Dr. James Connell, Director of the Institute for Research and Reform in Education. The first is a draft of a paper by him and Adema Klem, titled "A Theories-Change Approach to Evaluating Investments in Education"

(1998). Dr. Connell is unusual for an educational researcher-evaluator in that he truly knows schools and their culture, a knowledge that prevents him from oversimplifying the major factors that any reform effort is obliged to consider and for which relevant data must be obtained if the fruits of that effort are to be fairly and systematically judged and conclusions drawn not be misleading. The relevance of that paper, which I assume will be published, for charter schools is obvious. I say that because the second paper he sent me explicitly acknowledges Dr. Connell's influence. The paper was authored by Kathleen McGree and commissioned by the Southwest Educational Developmental Laboratory in Austin, Texas. The report is titled "Charter Schools in New Mexico and Texas: Designs for School-Site Reform" (1998). It is an analysis of the approved *written* applications of charter schools in the two states. The paper is *at present* a confidential document from which I cannot quote. When it does, as it will, become a public document, it will give substantial confirmation to what I have said in these chapters.

CHAPTER 10

Concluding Emphases

The major purpose of the 1972 book and to a lesser extent of this one was to suggest that although varieties of new settings may appear to be and truly are very different kinds of organizations, they are very similar in terms of issues and problems with which the process of their creation confronts. The practical or "so what?" significances of those similarities and differences are of two kinds: repair and prevention. When events require that we explain why one new setting is not achieving its agreed-upon purposes while another new setting of the same type is, the explanation far more often than not is in terms of personalities, or lack of vision, or incompetence, or a lack of technical-professional knowledge, or some combination of all of these. That explanation may in part or in whole have validity, but one is left with the impression that the failed setting would have had a different fate if it had had the kinds of people in the more successful one. That impression or conclusion assumes that what we know about either setting is relatively comprehensive, i.e., that we have the kind of description relevant to the factors discussed in this book. That is not the case if only for one reason: what we know about either setting is always (in my experience) retrospective in nature, depending as that does on the frailties of memory. That is why the Manhattan Project is so unusual. Although most of what we know about it is retrospective, it derives from so many different types of sources and people so soon after the project was completed—allowing cross checking, availability of archival material and letters, filling in of gaps in the story—that we have an unusually comprehensive account of how, why, and by whom that project was launched. I would go so far as to say that the Manhattan Project is the best described instance of the creation of a setting. It is unfortunately the case that the Manhattan Project is conceived of only as a chapter in the history of science, albeit with enormous societal and world repercussions. Its significances for the creation of other types of settings are not perceived. There are "lessons" to be drawn from it relevant to the creation of diverse types of human settings, lessons that could act as a preventive to failure partial or complete.

There are several aspects of the creation of settings I wish to emphasize.

1. The before-the-beginning phase contains all of the seeds of issues concerning clarity of purpose and goals, the resources that will be required, relations with external individuals and agencies, governance-leadership, and time perspective. It is a phase seen as a "tooling up" one, but it is also a phase in which enthusiasm and optimism are obstacles to pursuit of these issues in a sober, dispassionate way; some of them may be seen as so easy or self-evident as not to require much thought, if any.
2. The basis on which leaders are self-selected or chosen is *ordinarily* not conducive to an examination of goodness of fit between the leader and the nature, purposes, and demands of the setting. That is especially problematic in the instance of a setting (as with charter schools) where the new setting is unfamiliar to everyone who will participate in that setting. Where there is that degree of unfamiliarity, the requirement of an appropriate leadership becomes more crucial and fateful. And if he, she (or they) underestimate the problem, the seeds of failure will soon be visible.
3. Governance is about more than rules, procedures, and decision making. However you define governance, it inevitably becomes a climate producer by which I mean that governance is experienced in different ways by different participants. That in itself is not a negative if those differences can be safely surfaced and discussed. It is when participants do not feel able or willing to articulate reactions or ideas which call aspects of that governance into question, to appear to be rocking the boat, that governance has the effect of eliminating challenges at the expense of hearing potentially valuable information. To confuse the appearance of agreement and commitment with the psychological reality of all or most of the participants is too often the indulgence of wishful thinking.
4. Points 2 and 3 have to be seen in the climate of a context that suffuses the before-the-beginning phase and the first year or so of a new setting. Optimism about the future alternates with subdued forebodings about obstacles to smooth sailing. Public display of confidence about means and ends masks uncertainties about these means and ends, especially about means. Myriads of detail compel attention and require time and force reconsideration of the criteria for what is an important and an unimportant detail; time becomes an enemy, it is implacable. Whereas it was expected that there would always be problems to be overcome, it was not expected that these problems would be as complicated and thorny as they are; the participants learn that they do not live in a controllable world and that becomes a major source of frustration taking attention and time away from what they consider their basic purposes. Whereas initially it seemed as if everyone had similar, if not identical, understandings about every important issue relevant to means and ends,

cracks in that agreement begin to appear, the implications of which tend to be unexplored or glossed over or even postponed for discussion until the setting is off and running. These are *some* of the features of climate that can instill the feeling that one is less acting upon the world and more being acted upon by that world. There are, of course, variations in climate. The point here is that little or nothing in the creation of a setting should be seen as independent of climate.

It is understandable to me if readers of this book would conclude that if given the opportunity to create a new setting, they should decline. I, therefore, must caution the reader that what I have written was stimulated by the question: Why do so many new settings fall so short of the mark, or are total failures, or are aborted before they are functionally in existence? I am sure there are and have been settings that have been successful by my criteria. Very few of them have been described with the comprehensiveness and sensitivity providing us a basis for understanding their success. (So, for example, we know far more about dysfunctional marriages than functional ones.) That is why charter schools are theoretically and practically so important for the creation of settings. The concept of a charter school speaks to the perception of a national problem, i.e., the inadequate performance and outcomes of the traditional school in a traditional system. Charter schools represent the most radical critique of existing schools. What charter schools will demonstrate, for good or for bad, is a difference that will make a big difference. It is apparent from everything I have written about schooling that I am in favor of the concept of charter schools. It is not a perverse oppositional tendency on my part that causes me to be very pessimistic about what they will, generally speaking, demonstrate. It is rather that these schools have no conceptual "road map" to sensitize them to and to help them prepare for and overcome (partially at least) the predictable problems they will encounter. I did not write this book to serve as a kind of wet blanket to dampen the fires of enthusiasm in those who seek to create a setting. My purpose was more practical, but it is a purpose yet to be taken seriously. My present frame of mind is captured in my favorite Jewish joke. It is about the journalist assigned to the Jerusalem bureau of his newspaper. He got an apartment overlooking the Wailing Wall. After several weeks he became aware that regardless of when he looked at the wall, he saw this old Jew praying vigorously. There might be a story here, he thought, and he went down and said to the old Jew, "You pray every day at the wall. What do you pray for?" The old man replied, "What do I pray for? First I pray for world peace, then I pray for the brotherhood of man, and then I pray for the eradication of illness and disease from the world." The journalist was taken in with the man's sincerity and passion.

"You mean you come every day to the wall to pray for these three won-derful things." The old Jew nodded. The journalist asked, "How long have you been coming to the wall to offer these prayers," to which the old Jew said, "How long? Maybe 20, 25 years." The journalist was flabbergasted. "You mean you have come all those years to the wall to pray for these things?" The old Jew nodded. "How does it feel to have come all these years to the wall to offer these prayers?" The old Jew replied, "How does it feel? It is like talking to a wall."

CHAPTER 11

Postscripts and Signals

It should be clear from the previous chapters that my pessimism about the success of charter schools was based less on empirical data than on a rationale for the creation of settings I wrote more than a quarter of a century ago. Not only are there very little empirical data, but none is likely to be forthcoming. But in the last several months I became aware of several news articles that I do not offer as "data" but as signals that my pessimism may be justified.

1. In the *New York Times* of December 26, 1997, there is an article with the headline "Los Angeles Charter School Teachers Face Loss of Benefits." In 1993 the teachers in five charter schools had been granted leaves of absence by the school district so they could join the charter schools. Those leaves are ending, and the teachers must decide if they will quit the district and remain in the charter schools. If they choose to stay in the charter schools, they will forfeit seniority, tenure, and the district's lifetime health benefits. I have to assume that there is more here than meets the eye. One might ask why this issue was not anticipated. One also might ask if the issue reflects the opposition of groups who were or are opposed to charter schools, who have a vested interest in maintaining the school system as it now is, who see charter schools as threats. I doubt that it is only a money or resource issue, just as I doubt that these schools were created without engendering any opposition from within the district. The article does say that the teachers are lobbying district and union officials for an immediate one-year extension and amended contracts so they can remain for as long as the charter schools are open. Teacher unions have at best been ambivalent about charter schools and at worst opposed to them because they are, so to speak, loose cannons not easy to control. School district officials have never advocated for charter schools because they see charter schools from a zero-sum game stance: what these schools are given, the existing system loses.

2. In the *New York Times* for January 1, 1998, the headline for a news article is "Charter School Imperiled by Surprise Resignations." The principal and three of its four staff members (presumably teachers) resigned because the school (in New Jersey) with 24 sixth graders was understaffed

and the school board had repeatedly ignored requests to hire a specialist for two special-needs students. We are not told whether the number of staff was what was asked for in the application for charter school status. Nor are we told whether in the application there was recognition that there would or should be special-needs students. Was the request for an additional staff member "repeatedly ignored" because the school had been given what it asked for, or because (again) the school system did not look favorably on charter schools, or both? There is no point to playing the game of blame assignment. But it is to the point to say, as I have in previous chapters, that the concept of charter schools is too important and complex not to receive the searching description and scrutiny it deserves.

   3. In the op-ed page of the *New York Times* of January 2, 1998, Professor Gary Orfield of the Harvard Graduate School of Education calls attention to the troubles besetting charter schools in Arizona, Michigan, and Los Angeles.[1] Misuse of public funds, inadequate programs, ignoring the rights of students who need instruction in English as a second language, discriminating against special needs children and those who have no transportation to get to a charter school—these are points which lead Professor Orfield to title his article "Charter Schools Will Not Save Education." Instead, he advocates capitalizing on 20 years of experience with magnet schools and schools much smaller than the modal school today, and refers to a San Francisco school that was boldly reconstituted within existing old buildings. He concludes by saying that "success stories like those don't guarantee the equal distribution of educational opportunity that our public school system sorely needs. But these approaches at least permit major reforms without the risks or the limitations of the charter process." In my experience, and my reading of the literature, there is no credible evidence that magnet schools, even smaller schools, are sustained success stories. A minority of them appear to be successes, but in each case the most significant factor seems to be a level and quality of individual leadership that is in very short supply in our school systems, and there is no reason to believe that these systems are willing and able to increase the supply, let alone to seek out and support such leaders. We are in the dark

---

   1. Within 2 years after the passage of its charter school legislation, Arizona approved 167 charter schools, one third of the nation's total. I have a small collection of newspaper articles (*Wall Street Journal, Arizona Republic, Phoenix Gazette*) which is, to say the least, not pleasant reading for Arizona citizens. At least in my experience, the level of fiscal, moral, and educational chicanery in a fair number of Arizona's charter schools is *atypical* among charter schools in other states. I visit in Arizona yearly, enough to know that its political officialdom has cornered the market on ideology at the expense of caution and wisdom. Political officialdom in other states have cornered the market on caution and good intentions informed by ignorance, as I will elaborate on later.

when it comes to explaining why some magnet schools are successful and others are not. And, as I have emphasized, we are and will be in the dark when it comes to explaining why some charter schools will be successful and most of them will not be. I agree with Professor Orfield that charter schools will not save education, but the point of my argument in this book is that the charter school movement was doomed because it had a totally superficial, unrealistic conception of what is involved in creating a new setting. Professor Orfield mentions no successful charter school, or one that appears to be successful. I think Professor Orfield would agree that there are or will be successful charter schools. Just as we have much to learn from successful and unsuccessful magnet schools, we have much to learn from successful and unsuccessful charter schools. I venture the pre-diction that what we will learn from both is the crucial significance of bold, inspiring, street-smart leadership which does not confuse hope with real-ity, resources with money, productive learning with test scores, rhetoric with accomplishment, and knows the difference between principle and self-defeating compromise. If I do not agree with some of Professor Orfield's conclusions, I certainly respect his courage to criticize a movement which presents itself as savior. Education has had too many well-intentioned saviors whose capacity to oversimplify was bottomless.

4. In the *New York Times* of January 22, 1998, is an article with the headline "Whitman Backs Charter School Expansion." The occasion for Governor Whitman's announcement was a visit to a charter school in Princeton. The school, like 13 others that had also opened in the fall of 1997, was in a $2.8-million-dollar building paid for by private donations and loans from parents. The article goes on to say that the other charter schools were struggling with cramped buildings, transportation problems, and hostile local officials who complain that these schools are taking funds away from regular schools. In fact, most of the article, which takes up one quarter of a page, is devoted to the hostility expressed by school officials and boards of education toward charter schools. The article makes refer-ence to the charter school (discussed in 2 above) from which the princi-pal and three of the four teachers had resigned. One can assume that the Princeton charter school has no resource problems! The governor toured the school, admired a roomful of new computers, and she spoke French with the students, proclaiming "there is nothing more exciting than being in a charter school like this." Would she have said that if she toured the other charter schools? I feel justified in assuming that Governor Whitman knows that none of the other charter schools is at all compa-rable to the Princeton one, and it is highly likely that she knows the other schools are in trouble. If she knows that, why is she seeking to create 23 more charter schools without ascertaining the sources of the troubles all

but the Princeton school are experiencing? We should not overlook the fact that the charter schools which have opened were allowed to do so after their applications had been screened, judged, and approved. I would bet and give odds that those applications would reveal that the applications had a most unrealistic conception of what resources they would need and the hostility they would encounter from school officials. And it is too much to expect that those in the state department of education who evaluated the applications were any more sophisticated than those who wrote the applications and, therefore, could not helpfully sensitize them to what they were getting into. And, yet, Governor Whitman seeks to support more charter schools. That is why I titled my recent book *Political Leadership and Educational Failure* (1998). Political leaders have the obligation to learn what they can about a new educational policy, to go beyond what seems to be a good idea, and then to provide the means to evaluate the idea on the level of real action in the real world. Are political leaders exempt from those obligations? When things go badly with a new educational policy, who will they blame or scapegoat? There are groups, some of them passionate advocates for charter schools, who would not feel badly if our schools go downhill or out of existence. Who will they blame when and if studies indicate that, generally speaking, charter schools have fallen far short of their mark? But such studies will not be done, just as the number of credible studies for any reform effort have been pitifully small.

In 1996 *Charter Schools: Creating Hope and Opportunity for American Education*, by Joe Nathan, was published. As the subtitle suggests, the tone of the book is very upbeat. I am not opposed to motherhood, hope, and opportunity. Candor requires that I say that Nathan's book ignores the most important issues. Since his book was published in 1996, it was probably begun and completed in 1994–95 when the enthusiasm for charter schools was at its height and there were few or no clouds on the horizon. My negative assessment of the book may, therefore, be unfair.[2]

As I said in earlier chapters, I greeted the early stirrings of the charter school movement favorably but forebodingly. Favorably because the concept of a charter school was an *implicit and unarticulated* recognition that

---

2. In the March 16, 1998, *New York Times* there is an article about a study of charter schools by the Center for School Change at the University of Minnesota where Professor Nathan is director. Methodologically the study is seriously flawed. Ten of the 31 schools did not submit full results or any results at all; data were obtained by questionnaires and telephone calls; and the Center had no way of knowing if negative data were withheld. Professor Orfield is quoted as saying that "all you can conclude from this is that good schools that people nominate as good schools report that they are doing good." I agree. This footnote was appended after this book was in production.

our educational systems were incapable of self-correction or self-improvement, that if you wanted to move in new directions with new ideas, you had to be outside of the system. Forebodingly because there was obviously no rationale to serve as guide and warning for what the creation of new settings predictably and inevitably would confront. I hesitated to write about my concerns for two reasons. First, my past writings are viewed in some quarters as those of an academic Henny-Penny who only sees dark, threatening storms on the horizon. Second, in terms of data there was nothing to confirm my fears. Only a few charter schools had come into existence with much fanfare and approval, as if hope and the best of intentions were sufficient to overcome whatever potholes would be encountered. But the more I talked to people who were involved in some way with charter schools, and the more I learned about the "before the beginning" phases of these schools, and the more I learned about what seemed to be happening once these schools became operational, I felt justified to put my views in writing. For example, a colleague of mine, Dr. David Blumenkrantz, serves as consultant to some Connecticut charter schools, and he became interested in what was happening generally in the state's charter schools. He wrote me a long letter which contained the following. The letter is dated January 17, 1998.

> I am very concerned about the charter schools initiative in Connecticut. There seems to be a pattern emerging of consistent negative and unforeseen consequences. Also, the State Department of Education seems to be taking a laissez-faire attitude and thus far has done little to provide technical assistance or support to nurture these new educational settings. In fact, they just put together and distributed a list of school directors so they could get together. There is very little consideration for supporting the creation of these new settings and helping to confront the many challenges inherent in this venture.
>
> It seems somewhat ludicrous to think that innovations or experimentation in anything can be done economically. Extremely modest contributions for start-up were obtained exclusively from federal funds to initiate Charter Schools. Ongoing per pupil support obtained from State reimbursement is just over the minimum expenditure requirement (MER) by state law. One question could be asked: In the absence of Federal money to initiate Charter Schools would the State have gotten into the Charter School business? What was in the minds of those running the State Department of Education when they entered into the Charter School business? On one hand the state provided a conduit for Federal money which encouraged the creation of Charter Schools, on the other hand it makes available marginal per pupil financial supports (only 5% above the MER). I am aware that more than 50% of the Charter Schools presently have such significant financial problems that some of them may not be in business by next year. And I think

this is a conservative estimate! Part of the problem lies in the inadequacy of start-up funding for building renovation, rent, purchase of supplies, furniture, and equipment and real understanding of the organizational needs and personnel cost. Another part of the problem resides in the marginal per pupil expenditure support provided by the State. These two points demonstrate either a complete lack of understanding of what it takes to create innovations in education or an extremely limited commitment to their success.

The funding situation is exacerbated by Charter Schools being between the proverbial rock and a hard place. The rock: It is no secret that the State of Connecticut has underfunded the Charter Schools. In fact, one of the largest private charitable foundations in the state made a policy decision not to make contributions to any Charter School. They felt that the State's start-up funding was so inadequate that they were not going to assume responsibility for "carrying" these educational innovations. A majority of the private charitable foundations that could have played a significant role followed the lead of this large foundation, eliminating many potential sources of funding. The hard place: State teacher organizations lobbied hard against Charter Schools. These "non union shops" presented unacceptable competition to unions who pressured the legislature to reduce the amount of state start-up money.

Directors and trustees of charter schools are being consumed by these life-and-death funding problems. As a result the process of growing these educational innovations is being stunted. While the founders of these Charters could not have anticipated all of the problems that lay ahead, they were completely unprepared for the economic realities that were closing in on them. It was like a family that wanted a lot of children but did not have enough money to feed them. How do you make the decision which child does not get fed? The financial situation has become the most pressing problem for a majority of Charters. The State Department of Education, who is administering the Charter grant initiative, does not seem to be playing a significant role through technical assistance and support. They have done little to link the key administrators of Charter Schools, a potential for resource and knowledge exchange. While they put up the initiating funds, they seem to be remaining in the background providing the investment without reasonable responsibility. And, while they have contracted with the National Evaluation Center to do a five-year study of charters, they have overlooked the challenges of start-up. By the time the Evaluation Centers survey materials are put in place the "whole shooting match" may be over.

The next series of challenges revolve around what I call "carrying through with the vision." It is one thing to imagine what a wonderful school would look like. It is quite another to deal with the reality of constructing one from scratch and managing its growth. Does the birth and care of new Charter Schools come with an instruction manual? The State Department of Education certainly didn't supply one. While literature exists on the formation of Charters, I'm not sure those who envisioned "their" schools had much appreciation of this literature.

Who are these people who "envisioned" and wrote the proposals for Charters? And, what were their qualifications to run these new educational experiments? From my limited vantage point it appears that those who envisioned the school and are now directing their creation, while nice, bright, well-meaning people, had neither the experience or skills to administer these new complicated ventures. They also did not have the administrative support that should be present for any start-up organization's success. Financial, secretarial, purchasing, phone and computer installation, lighting and electrical engineering were all responsibilities confronting these new administrators. Besides they were supposed to be guiding the educational innovation, developing curriculum, engaging parents and community representatives, hiring teachers, etc. . . . . It has been overwhelming, to understate the obvious. Again, much of the administrative complexities have been magnified by limited funding, which was not available, to bring on resources to manage some of these issues.

Who are the parents and children that are enrolling in these educational experiments? And, why would anyone take a risk with their child's educational development on these experiments? I'm sure there are as many answers to these questions as parents and children enrolled. There does seem to be some interesting similarities from which several generalizations can be suggested. First, parents were generally dissatisfied with and were looking for a different educational setting then public education. Second, children were not doing well, for a variety of reasons, in public school. Third, parents wanted greater input into their child's education. These situations precipitate unforeseen consequences. Some of the children's special education needs were completely unanticipated and, to a certain extent, overwhelmed the new school. In one school the majority of students enrolled were at risk of dropping out of their previous schools and were identified as having special education needs. The new charter schools were not equipped to respond to the special education needs of many of their students. On the other hand parents who wanted greater involvement in their child's schooling were a formidable group to work with. Some of them had a long history of very negative relationships with public schools. They were very aggressive and domineering in their desire to be involved, or more aptly stated, be in control of the schools. Of course, many students were there for the "right" reasons, to excel and be challenged by better educational opportunities.

Suffice it to say that in the midst of trying to design and implement educational innovations, to set up the physical space and administrative organization for a new educational setting, the intensity of parent involvement presented another set of challenges. While the creators of these new settings may have given considerable thought to problems of education, they may not have considered the significant impact of parents and the community. As one Director said: "These schools were wonderful places until the students and parents showed up."

Who are the people who work in these new settings? And what history and skills do they have which makes them suited for these challenges? Since there were relatively fewer requirements than public schools for certified teachers, a broad array of people with differing experiences and skills seem to be employed in these new settings. It is too early to say whether their exuberance and dedication will outweigh their inexperience. These people bring a new meaning to "on the job training." In part their dedication to the new educational setting may allow a greater degree of flexibility which is very much in demand. This is an area that needs considerable investigation and would have significant implications for the training, certification, and collective bargaining of teachers. For example: what are the implications of the success of Charter Schools, given the lenient stance for certification and other union requirements?

What is the most important *practical* question political leaders should ask when they adopt an educational policy they hope will lead to meaningful, long overdue reform, such as charter schools? That first practical question is: Do charter schools have the educational outcomes for which the policy was adopted? Do they work as intended, as hoped for? The first question is not a financial one: Can those outcomes be obtained for x or y amount of funding, or the same amount of funding given to existing schools whose inadequacies the new policy recognizes? The first question is whether charter schools will achieve their purposes if given the resources they need even if those resources will require funding beyond that given to existing schools, especially if the new policy is about schools foreign to everyone's experience? How do you determine level of funding when you have no experience to serve as a guide? As I said earlier in this book, I am not suggesting that charter schools be given a blank check but rather that one has to be prepared to increase funding depending on what one learns from the first cohort of charter schools. What Dr. Blumenkrantz has observed about "resources" is what I have personally observed, or read, or about which I have been told. One would expect that the policy makers are making it their business to learn what is going on and why, but that is not the case at all. They adopted a policy in a publicly self-congratulatory way, then arbitrarily decided on level of funding, and are learning nothing because they did not include means by which they could learn how to improve the chances for success of the new policy. It is an old story: The more things change the more they remain the same.

Relevant to the above is a 3-day visit I recently made to a charter school in January 1998 in Chandler, Arizona. It may well be that Arizona has given approval to more charter schools than any other three states combined. It is probably also the case that, as Professor Orfield (1998) suggests in his op-ed article in the *New York Times*, that a fair number of these Arizona charter schools are in deep trouble; some have already died an early death, in part because of fiscal chicanery.

The charter school I visited was sponsored by the Ball Foundation in Illinois. I had known Mr. Ball and Dr. Steven Goldman (executive director) for a number of years and met several times with them. Although I did not agree with some of their plans and activities, I had not the faintest doubt that their concerns and criticisms of school reform efforts were right on target. I learned about their initiative in Chandler, a suburb of Phoenix, in the spring of 1997. The school opened in September 1997, and my visit with an assistant, Dr. Irma Miller, took place 5 months later. Before going there we knew or were told the following:

1. Getting the charter from the state was no big deal but, once obtained, different groups, individuals, and city authorities raised numerous problems and obstacles. The school was to be housed in an unused Korean church in a residential neighborhood, and questions were raised about whether the building met safety and structural regulations, whether undesirable, unsafe traffic patterns would be created, whether sidewalks and access to the school were adequate, and more. The Ball Foundation obtained legal counsel in regard to how to deal with various city departments each of which had raised objections that would be costly, very costly.
2. We had been sent a video of a city council meeting at which the public had opportunity to give its views. It is evident from the video that those who expressed their views said not a word about the educational program but only objected to what the presence of the school might do to the neighborhood. Viewing the video it is hard to avoid the conclusion that although the Ball Foundation had already reached agreement with the city agencies on most issues, there were individuals and groups whose unarticulated aim was to prevent approval of anything that would upset the status quo.
3. Aside from the per pupil expenditure ($4,164) from the state, the foundation "donates" $2,000 for each student. This is in addition to approximately several hundred thousand dollars expended to meet all requirements of the different city agencies.
4. The school has several distinctive goals. The first is a "total immersion" foreign language program which means that English is not spoken in foreign language classes (which meet twice a week). The second is an emphasis on technology and phonics. The third is that significant time is devoted to staff development, which is not confused with one-day workshops or taking more courses.
5. The school operates on a 210-day calendar.
6. The initial cohort in this K-8 school consisted of 190 students, which included a fair number of students with special needs.

7. The principal of the school is Nancy Helm, who had previously been head of one of the three state agencies with power to approve the creation of a charter school. (This is why getting a charter in Arizona has been relatively easy, an ease which as Professor Orfield rightly notes, has not been without occasional unfortunate consequences.)

I was eager to visit the school, but I did not have high expectations. Although we gained an overall impression of the school, a very favorable one, I do not feel justified on the basis of the 3-day visit to conclude that Chandler is or will be a success story. That this 5-month-old school opened on time, took in 190 students, and is a relaxed, humming place—despite its "before the beginning" stormy, obstacle-ridden stage—is a long story many details of which we did not have time to ferret out. What I feel secure in reporting are several observations and events which are the basis of our favorable impression, and which will give the reader some basis for judgment, however tentative those judgments should be.

The first observation concerns the principal, Nancy Helm. That she is a dynamo is an understatement. More important, she has a clear sense of priorities: teachers have to be stimulated, supported, listened to; the individual needs of students and parents should never be ignored or glossed over, however time consuming and frustrating their problems may be; parents have a role to play in classrooms, they are an educational resource; teachers can and should be resources to each other and that includes some teachers who do not have formal credentials; you do what you have to do to deal with problems even if it requires departing from conventional practice; she expected the school to have growing pains, to have crises, but her responsibility was to make sure those pains and crises had to be squarely and publicly confronted. We visited all classrooms. The eighth-grade classroom had a dozen or so students and a young, eager but relaxed teacher. What we observed were clusters of students each working on a particular problem about measuring distances on a map. They did not appear to be bored, they talked spontaneously but softly among themselves. If it was not the liveliest class we had ever seen, neither was it a deadening, stifling class of teenagers. The fact is that from day one this young, noncredentialed teacher had been unable to control and teach the class, some of whom had previously been labeled as behavior and learning problems. What Nancy Helm did, almost immediately, was to spend a solid block of time each day in that classroom "teaching" and supporting the young man who now is a competent, motivating teacher. She did that over several months.

During one of our discussions with Nancy Helm we asked her to describe the atmosphere in the weeks preceding and following opening of the schools. She replied (paraphrased), "We were not physically able to assemble as a group until a couple of weeks before opening. Some teachers moved here from other states. The long and short of it is that everyone worked from 12–15 hours a day, including weekends, getting to know each other, hammering out details about scheduling, curriculum issues, goals and philosophy, the role of parents, and God knows what else. And that included opening up crates of books and other materials, TVs, computers. And after the school opened a 12-hour day was the norm, and even today, 5 months after opening, these teachers are devoting a degree of time, energy, and commitment I regard as amazing, and I wonder how long they can go on this way. I am seriously considering asking the Ball Foundation to give the teachers a bonus. Their salaries are by no means high—salaries in Arizona generally are low—and they deserve some recognition for what they have accomplished and as a stimulus to them to continue as they are. You cannot take for granted that they will be able to give such time and energy without the danger of burnout."

Toward the end of the first day of our visit we requested a meeting with parents on the next day. They were able to round up a dozen parents who would be able to come. We opened the meeting by saying that we wanted to get some idea of how they saw the school and we hoped they would be as candid and helpful as possible. We went around the room asking each parent to respond. No one was silent or reticent. What each of them expressed was dissatisfaction with the previous schools their children had attended. Two (perhaps three) parents had special needs children; one parent had two such children both of whom were now at Chandler. Her voice trembled, she became tearful as she described her despair at the insensitivity of the previous school to her children's unhappiness and lack of achievement. She then went on to describe how by the end of the first month at Chandler her children wanted to go to school, loved their teachers, and were beginning to learn. Chandler, she said, was like a miracle; the teachers were like a gift from God. Her account, which took about 10 minutes, brought tears to the eyes of some of the other parents whose own accounts were not as emotional or impactful but who told similar stories. Nancy Helm was at the meeting. Half way through it I asked the parents if what they were saying they had said to the teachers. The answers were no. I then asked Nancy Helm if what the parents had said was in the records of those children. The answer was no. The meeting continued but Nancy left the room. We learned later that she had gone to her office and circulated a memo to all teachers in which she told them (a) how the parents regarded them and (b) how proud she was of them and they should be of themselves. I have over the decades met with many small groups of parents, albeit in different circumstances and for different reasons, but in almost all cases parental satisfaction or dissatisfaction with teachers and schooling could have been expressed. But no meeting had the compellingness of the Chandler one.

When we spoke to the teachers individually, asking them to tell us about their classrooms and students, one feature stood out: Without prompting on our part, at some point each teacher illustrated what she wanted to convey by describing one or more students who required some change in teaching tactics, or had talents and interests the teacher had not known about, or about whom parents had asked questions the teacher then sought to answer by more systematic observation of the child. (Each teacher had already made one home visit for each of his or her students.) We were impressed, frankly surprised, at how seriously individuality was taken.

Finally, the Ball Foundation hired a highly respected and well known anthropologist-ethnographer, Dr. Donna Muncey, to observe and record the developmental history of the school. I know of no other instance where the means for a longitudinal study of a charter school was provided so as to make possible that at some point we will have a basis for identifying factors contributing to whatever degree of success or failure the school will demonstrate.

The main reason I have discussed the Chandler school has to do with the reported difficulties charter schools are having with issues of resources. Political leaders and other charter school advocates have illogically, shortsightedly, and arbitrarily proceeded on two assumptions. First, charter schools are not only needed alternatives to regular schools but if they are successful they can bring about a meaningful transformation of schools generally. As I indicated earlier, I agree with that assumption. It is the second assumption that makes no practical sense: Charter schools will be judged successes or failures if they can achieve their purposes with the same resources existing schools have, even though the policy makers know full well that the billions upon billions of dollars spent on school improvement in the post-World War II era have far from achieved their purposes. If money was the answer, schools should be dramatically better than they are. The fundamental question that charter school advocates did not have the wisdom or courage to confront was: What resources might or would a charter school require to determine whether it can serve as a basis for future policy? That, as I have said earlier, does not mean that legislators write a blank check, but it does mean that if charter schools are as potentially important as their advocates assert, should we not give or be prepared to give them more per-pupil costs than regular schools get? The first question that has to be answered is do they, generally speaking, achieve their purposes and, if they do, what are the economic implications for changing existing schools? To arbitrarily answer the resource question before there is any secure basis for doing so is truly to put the cart before the horse. The Manhattan Project (Chapter 7) was not asked to meet its goal with a predetermined budget cap because what the times demanded was an answer to the question: Was an atomic bomb a practical possibility? In its own way, and up to a point, that is the question the Ball Foundation seeks to answer at Chandler. The resources of the foundation are limited, it cannot and will not write blank checks. But despite those obvious limitations the foundation is providing resources that permits us to say that Chandler is not being starved. It deserves reiterating that the near-universal complaint of charter schools centers around inadequate resources. Having said that, I remind the reader that the thrust of this book is that resources were but one factor among several that has led me to predict that charter schools will be another chapter in the history of flawed educational reform efforts.

But one does not have to look at charter schools from my perspective to predict that they will reveal serious problems. All one needs to know is that the concept of the charter school is new and untried and, therefore, that its implementation will have many "bugs." How many years of hard work and repeated failures did it take the Wright brothers to construct a plane that would stay aloft for more than a few seconds? And how many years of learning, of experimentation, of drudgery and persistence, did it take Edison to come up with his major inventions. One could argue that Edison and the Wright brothers were dealing with things, not people and human institutions. True. But that argument concedes the point: Although reinventing and changing a traditional organization can be expected to be enormously more complicated, it still will require an approach which starts with an initial model, develops a second and improved model, on and on in a process of continuous improvement, a process described by Wilson and Daviss (1994). I know of no educational policy in the post-World War II era that has been implemented on that basis. The charter school movement is, unfortunately, the latest chapter in that saga.

References

Atzmon, E. (1958). The educational programs for immigrants in the United States. *History of Education Journal, 9*(3), 75–80.

Augustine, N. (1997, May-June). Reshaping an industry: Lockheed-Martin's survival story. *Harvard Business Review*, pp. 83–96.

Blumenkrantz, D.G. (1992). *Fulfilling the promise of children's services.* San Francisco: Jossey-Bass.

Burns, J. A. (1969). *The growth and development of the Catholic school system in the United States.* New York: Arno Press, New York Times.

Cherniss, C. (1972). *New settings in the university: Their creation, problems, and early development.* Unpublished doctoral dissertation, Yale University.

Connell, J., & Klem, A. (1998). *A theories-change approach to evaluating investments in education.* Unpublished manuscript, Institute for Research and Reform in Education, 308 Glendale Drive, Toms River, NJ 08753.

Cowden, P., & Cohen, D. (n.d.). *Divergent worlds of practice. The federal reform of local schools in the Experimental Schools Program.* Available from Dr. Peter Cowden, c/o Transitions, Solutions, Inc., 177 Worcester Road, Route 9W, Wellesley Hills, MA 02181.

Grouett, S. (1968). *Manhattan Project.* Boston: Little Brown.

Holland, B. (1997, July 20). A music Mecca loved but reluctantly. *New York Times.*

Holsinger, M. P. (1968). The Oregon school bell controversy, 1922–25. *Pacific Historical Review*, 327–341.

Jorgenson, L. P. (1968). The Oregon School Law of 1922: Passage and sequel. *Catholic Historical Review, 54*, 455–466.

Kammerand-Campbell, S. (1989). *Doc: The story of Dennis Littky and his fight for a better school.* Chicago: Contemporary Books.

Louis, K. S., & King, J. A. (1993). Professional cultures and reforming schools. Does the myth of Sisyphus apply? In J. Murphy & P. Hallinger (Eds.), *Restructuring Schooling* (pp. 216–250). Newbury Park, CA: Corwin Press.

McGree, K. (1998). *Charter schools in New Mexico and Texas: Designs for school site reform.* Unpublished manuscript, Southwest Educational Developmental Laboratory, Austin, Texas.

Minnesota charter schools evaluation: An interim report. (1996). Minneapolis: University of Minnesota Center for Applied Research and Educational Improvement.

Moynihan, D. P. (1969). *Maximum feasible misunderstanding.* New York: Free Press.

Nathan, J. (1996). *Charter schools: Creating hope and opportunity.* San Francisco: Jossey-Bass.

O'Brien, K. B. (1961). Education, Americanization, and the Supreme Court: The 1920's. *American Quarterly, 13*(2), 161–171.

Orfield, D. (1998, January 2). Charter schools will not save education. *New York Times* (Op-ed page).

Rhodes, R. (1988). *The making of the atomic bomb.* New York: Simon and Schuster.

Sarason, S. B. (1972). *The creation of settings and the future societies.* San Francisco: Jossey-Bass.

Sarason, S. B. (1988). *The making of an American psychologist.* San Francisco: Jossey-Bass.

Sarason, S. B. (1990). *The predictable failure of educational reform.* San Francisco: Jossey-Bass.

Sarason, S. B. (1993a). *The case for change. Rethinking the preparation of educators.* San Francisco: Jossey-Bass.

Sarason, S. B. (1993b). *Letters to a serious education president.* Newbury, CA: Corwin Press.

Sarason, S. B. (1993c). *You are thinking of teaching?* San Francisco: Jossey-Bass.

Sarason, S. B. (1995). *Parental involvement and the political principle.* San Francisco: Jossey-Bass.

Sarason, S. B. (1996). *Revisiting "The culture of the school and the problem of change."* New York: Teachers College Press.

Sarason, S. B. (1997). *How schools might be governed and why.* New York: Teachers College Press.

Sarason, S. B. (1998). *Political leadership and educational failure.* San Francisco: Jossey-Bass.

Sarason, S. B., & Lorentz, E. (1997). *Coordination: Process, problems, and opportunities in schools, private sector, and federal government.* San Francisco: Jossey-Bass.

Stakes, A. P., & Pfeffer, L. (1950). *Church and state in the United States: Historical development and contemporary problems of religious freedom under the constitution* (Volumes 1–3). New York: Harper and Brothers.

Thompson, F. V. (1971). *Americanization studies. Volume 1: Schooling of the immigrant.* Montclair, NJ: Patterson-Smith.

Tyack, D. B. (1968). The perils of pluralism: The background of the Pierce Case. *American Historical Review, 46,* 355–389.

Tyack, D. B. (1976). Ways of seeing: An essay on the history of compulsory schooling. *Harvard Educational Review, 46,* 355–389.

Weiss, A. R. (1997). *Going it alone.* Boston: Institute for Responsive Education, Northeastern University.

Wilson, K., & Daviss, B. (1994). *Redesigning education.* New York: Teachers College Press.

About the Author

Seymour B. Sarason is professor of psychology emeritus in the Department of Psychology and at the Institution for Social and Policy Studies of Yale University. In 1962 he founded and directed the Yale Psycho-Educational Clinic, one of the first research and training sites in community psychology. Fields in which he has made special contributions include mental retardation, culture and personality, projective techniques, teacher training, anxiety in children, and school reform. His numerous books and articles reflect his broad interests.

Dr. Sarason received his Ph.D. degree from Clark University in 1942 and holds honorary doctorates from Syracuse University, Queens College, Rhode Island College, and Lewis and Clark College. He has received awards from the American Psychological Association and the American Association on Mental Deficiency.